10 Blessings of God
You Won't Want To Miss

With Study Guide

Susan Barnes

Dedicated to Rev. Stewart Rae

1937–2023

Bible Teacher, Worship Leader, Pastor

I'm so much richer because of all he taught me.

Copyright © 2025 by Susan Barnes

First published in Australia by Reams of Grace Pty Ltd

US Edition

ISBN: 978-1-7641202-0-3

 A catalogue record for this book is available from the National Library of Australia

Unless otherwise indicated, all Scripture quotations are taken from the *Holy Bible*, New Living Translation, copyright © 1996, 2004, 2015 by Tyndale House Foundation. Used by permission of Tyndale House Publishers, Carol Stream, Illinois 60188. All rights reserved.

Scripture quotations marked (NIV) are taken from the New International Version® NIV® Copyright © 1973, 1978, 1984, 2011 by Biblica, Inc. Used with permission. All rights reserved worldwide.

Scripture quotations marked (MSG) are taken from *The Message*, copyright © 1993, 2002, 2018 by Eugene H. Peterson. Used by permission of NavPress. All rights reserved. Represented by Tyndale House Publishers.

Scripture quotations marked (AMPC) are taken from the Amplified® Bible (AMPC), Copyright © 1954, 1958, 1962, 1964, 1965, 1987 by The Lockman Foundation. Used by permission. lockman.org.

Scripture quotations marked (NKJV) are taken from the New King James Version®. Copyright © 1982 by Thomas Nelson. Used by permission. All rights reserved.

All rights reserved. No part of this publication may be reproduced in any form, stored in a retrieval system, or transmitted in any form by any means—electronic, photocopy, recording, or otherwise—except for brief quotations in reviews, without prior written permission of the publisher.

Contents

Introduction	3
God Shares His Happiness	5
God Surprises	23
God Frees	39
God Identifies with Us	55
God Loves	71
God Gives Hope	87
God Has a Plan	103
God Blesses	119
God Gives Peace	135
God Overcomes	151
Conclusion	167

Introduction

Do God's blessings make a practical difference in your daily life?

Isaiah prophesies that God's people will be known as a blessed people. "Everyone will realize that they are a people the Lord has blessed" (Isaiah 61:9). When people look at our lives do they notice something different about us because God has blessed us?

Through this book, I hope to motivate you to chase after God's blessings. God wants to bless us more than we want to be blessed. I have pondered this thought a great deal, as it was often said by Rev. Stewart Rae when I attended the church where he was the senior pastor. Stewart's insightful preaching had an enormous impact on my life.

The problem with God's willingness to bless is it can make the recipient feel vulnerable, inadequate, or incompetent. Some would rather toughen up and act like they don't need God. Or they'd rather God bless them just a little bit, enough to have an easy life but not so much that it makes them feel uncomfortable.

But that's not how God works.

Jesus says to Peter, "Now go out where it is deeper, and let down your nets to catch some fish" (Luke 5:4). The resulting catch is so large that it nearly sinks two boats (v. 7). The experience is life-changing. Peter leaves everything and follows him (v. 11).

God desires to bless his people but not necessarily for their hard work or devotion. "Anyone who wants to come to him must believe that God exists and that he rewards those who sincerely seek him" (Hebrews 11:6). God wants us to believe we will be blessed or rewarded for seeking him. Faith isn't entirely altruistic.

Gideon has a transformative encounter with God and calls him "The Lord is peace" (Judges 6:24). But this happens before God miraculously defeats the enemy. God desires to bless us with peace that is life-changing.

Supposing God blesses us in a life-changing way?

It's easy to become comfortable with our level of spirituality and grow dull to God's prompting to continue to seek him. Instead, let's be like Mary sitting at Jesus's feet (Luke 10:39, 42), like David thirsting for God (Psalm 42:2), and like Paul pressing on to possess all God has for him (Philippians 3:10–12). Until we are Christlike, God always has more for us—more joy, surprises, grace, empathy, love, hope, plans, blessings, peace, and victories. So many blessings you won't want to miss. The Christian life is exciting because God always has something more for us. If you're bored with the Christian life, you aren't living it as God intended.

I pray as you read these words, you will hear God calling you to a deeper place of relationship with him. The blessings of God come to those who have an open heart and open hands to receive them. I hope this book gives you a fresh perspective on God's goodness. I pray you will encounter him in new ways as you respond to his call and you're open to receiving his many blessings.

God bless,

Susan

1

God Shares His Happiness

Jesus is happy.

This thought didn't occur to me until I watched the Visual Bible recording of Matthew's gospel.[1] Even though I had been a Christian for quite a while, it surprised me to see the actor, Bruce Marchiano, portray Jesus as happy and laughing. One day, I rewatched the video with a young friend, who commented, "Jesus is always smiling." Perhaps I wasn't the only one surprised by a happy Jesus.

Does this accurately portray Jesus?

Marchiano wrote a book about his experience, called *In the Footsteps of Jesus*.[2] In it, he describes how he worked and prayed to portray Jesus as accurately as possible. Since God made us in his image, logically, God would have a sense of humor and the ability to see the lighter side of life. But I hadn't made the connection. I started looking for *happiness* and *joy* when I read the Bible, and suddenly they seemed to be everywhere:

> You will show me the way of life, granting me
> the joy of your presence and the pleasures of
> living with you forever. (Psalm 16:11)

> Though you do not see him now, you trust him; and you rejoice with a glorious, inexpressible joy. (1 Peter 1:8)
>
> The people of Judah and Israel were as numerous as the sand on the seashore; they ate, they drank and they were happy. (1 Kings 4:20 NIV)

Jesus's happiness and joy teaches us an important truth. If Jesus is happy, I can be happy too.

God is happy, and he invites us to share his happiness.

God is happy, relaxed, unflustered, at peace. The last page is written—evil will be conquered, and all God's people will live happily ever after. We can take such confidence from this.

Furthermore, he calls us to share his happiness. But will we?

Jesus, Happy and Joyful

With the work of the cross complete, Jesus is happy because he has won the victory over all the circumstances that would steal our happiness and joy. But why didn't I instinctively think of Jesus as happy?

Jesus is holy, and I thought holiness was a serious business, incompatible with happiness. The opposite is true. People can be truly happy only if they live law-abiding, responsible lives. People who are constantly in trouble with the police aren't happy. They're angry and frustrated, or depressed and anxious.

I thought Jesus couldn't be happy while sin still exists in the world. Jesus knows the devastation sin causes, yet he has dealt with this through his death and resurrection. One day, God will redeem all the effects of sin. Since sin is temporary, it doesn't stop Jesus from being happy. It doesn't have to stop me from being happy either.

Isaiah prophesies about Jesus's earthly ministry, "He was despised and rejected—a man of sorrows, acquainted with deepest grief" (Isaiah 53:3).

Jesus does have periods of pain and distress, so he isn't always happy. After all, he weeps at Lazarus's grave (John 11:35). Even now, he enters into our feelings of pain. "In all their distress he too was distressed" (Isaiah 63:9 NIV). God doesn't expect us to glue a smile on our faces, and he doesn't get angry with us if we're not happy. Nevertheless, joy is a fruit of the Spirit that, with maturity, will characterize our lives.

Based on Isaiah 53:3, some call Jesus "a man of sorrows," but this doesn't show the full picture of his time on earth. Other passages balance this view.

> I have told you these things so that you will be filled with my joy. Yes, your joy will overflow! (John 15:11)

> At that same time Jesus was filled with the joy of the Holy Spirit. (Luke 10:21)

While Jesus suffers, enduring the consequences of sin, even in this the writer of Hebrews tells us, "Because of the joy awaiting him, he endured the cross, disregarding its shame" (Hebrews 12:2).

Like Jesus, we can endure hardships because we have hope beyond our present circumstances.

Finally, I didn't think of Jesus as happy because not every Christian I've met is happy. I must admit, some days I'm not happy either. Even as a Christian, sometimes I experience a sense of hopelessness. Mostly, this happens when I feel overwhelmed by my circumstances. We relocated many times when our children were young. Moving into a new community, making new friends, and managing new work situations took their toll mentally and physically. At times, I found myself being sucked into despondency, even though I knew God "richly gives us all we need for our enjoyment" (1 Timothy 6:17).

God desires for me to enjoy my life. He asks me to share his happiness.

Christians ought to be the happiest people in the world, but God understands the challenges we face, and he desires to restore our hope. Jesus's happiness gives us abundant hope. I can be happy too. This also gives me immense security.

If Jesus sits at God's right hand with all power and authority, then who am I to be worried and upset?

If Jesus knows all there is to know and is happy, then who am I to disagree?

If Jesus is always with me, then who am I to waste my time feeling troubled?

God's Self-Portrait

When we look at Jesus's life in the Gospels, we see that crowds flock to hear him (Matthew 4:25), children want to be near him (Luke 18:16), and one man even climbs a tree (Luke 19:4). If Jesus were grumpy, frustrated, or irritable, people wouldn't want to be near him. This teaches us something significant about God's character, since Jesus is the exact representation of God (Hebrews 1:3).

If Jesus is happy, then God is too. Some can picture a happy Jesus but struggle with the image of a happy God.

When we open our Bibles and read about God's disappointment with Adam and Eve (Genesis 3:13), his flooding of the world in Noah's time (7:24), and his scattering of the people at the Tower of Babel (11:6–7), we may question the notion of a happy God. Yet when we look at the overarching theme of the Bible, we see that God has gone to enormous lengths to show us his character. God's intentions toward us are good—he sent Jesus. We have ample reason to celebrate his goodness and share his happiness.

The Bible is a collection of stories about God as he touched the lives of ordinary men and women in various ways and at various times. Through stories, God shows us what a relationship with him looks like.

God passionately desires a relationship with people.

Being in a relationship with his people brings God joy. He desires relationship, even though he doesn't need us (Acts 17:25). While God didn't create us with the sole purpose of making him happy or because he needed us to serve him or worship him, we bring him joy when we choose fellowship with him. He created us out of his abundance, not because of any shortfall. We don't walk around on eggshells trying to keep God happy. He's already happy. He's already fulfilled. He has everything he needs.

Good parents have children not to turn them into slaves but to share life with them. Likewise, God wants to share his life with us.

Becoming Happy

The world would tell us we will find happiness in accumulating possessions or achieving success. The truth is we'll never grow happy focusing on ourselves.

We become happy by worshiping God.

We don't worship God because he is vain. He doesn't need us to tell him he's good, worthy, or holy, but we benefit from the reminder. He doesn't need our assurance of his divine power and goodness, but we do. We worship to remind ourselves of spiritual realities, to remember the one who's on the throne. Whether we sing or pray or simply talk about God's attributes, we move the attention off ourselves and onto God.

I define worship as moving our attention off ourselves and placing it on God—to contemplate his character.

Unfortunately, just because I know this doesn't mean I always do it. At times I can sit through an entire church service, a Bible study, or a prayer time totally disengaged. My mind focuses on my own concerns, and God seems distant.

One of the things that has helped me focus is to imagine I'm hearing the message, or the Bible reading, or the song for the very first time. Sometimes we feel like we've heard it all before. But when we imagine we're hearing it for the first time, it can change our perspective.

God is worthy of all my consideration and all my time. When I worship, I acknowledge God as the most valuable being there is, who has given me what's most valuable, himself. When I focus on God, it heightens my awareness of his sovereignty and the smallness of my concerns. Worship helps me draw near to God. James tells us, "Come close to God, and God will come close to you" (James 4:8).

We worship so we can stop being the center of our attention.

Through times of worship at church or home, we stop obsessing about our needs and problems. We worship to reflect on God's place in our lives. And as we do, we become happy.

Many times, the psalmist exhorts us to praise God, which is the natural overflow of understanding God's greatness. Whenever something impresses us, we want to tell others and have them join us in our excitement.[3] We say to people:

"You must see this terrific movie."

"Wasn't last night's game amazing?"

"Isn't the sunset awesome?"

Likewise, the psalmist says:

> Come, *let us* sing to the Lord!
> *Let us* shout joyfully to the
> Rock of our salvation.
> *Let us* come to him with thanksgiving.
> *Let us* sing psalms of praise to him.
> For the Lord is a great God,
> a great King above all gods. ...
> Come, *let us* worship and bow down.
> *Let us* kneel before the Lord our maker,
> for he is our God.
> (Psalm 95:1–7, emphasis added)

The psalmist longs for others to join him in acknowledging the greatness of our God. In expressing our enthusiasm for God's goodness, our own joy deepens. John explains this process when he says, "We write this to make our joy complete" (1 John 1:4 NIV).

I'd expect him to say, "We write this to make your joy complete." But no, it's in expressing our own enthusiasm for God's goodness that our own joy is intensified and completed.

Joy Stealers

What prevents us from being happy?

Worry, fear, frustration, discontent, intimidation, trying to control our circumstances, or my personal favorite, sensing time is short and I'll die before I reach all my goals. I have a few writing projects in process, and sometimes I worry that I'll die before I finish writing everything I've started. What are the joy stealers in your life?

> The seed that fell among the thorns represents those who hear God's word, but all too quickly the message is crowded out by the worries of this life and the lure of wealth, so no fruit is produced. (Matthew 13:22)

Jesus describes "the worries of this life and the lure of wealth" as weeds choking the good seed. Worry robs us of joy, and so does the attraction of wealth. Some falsely believe money will solve all their problems, relieve them of their worries, and then they will be happy. Money isn't the answer, and God doesn't want us deceived into thinking it is. God doesn't want us to depend on material wealth to make us happy.

God's joy isn't affected by our joy stealers. He doesn't worry. He knows the future and doesn't waste time imagining worst-case scenarios or inventing contingencies for every emergency. He doesn't focus on what could go wrong. We deny ourselves peace and joy when we fill our minds with negative possibilities that might not even happen.

Neither is God caught by surprise. He never says, "Oh bother, I didn't think of that." Nothing frustrates God. No one can thwart his plans. "Our God is in the heavens, and he does as he wishes" (Psalm 115:3).

This thought alone makes me happy. God is in heaven. He's sovereign. And the things that please God are good. He longs to be gracious to us and show us his favor. He isn't alarmed by evil plans or the perverted ways of people's hearts. Nothing happens without his consent. Nothing catches him unawares. Nothing slips his notice.

When we look at Jesus's life, we see another joy stealer that doesn't move him—intimidation. The religious leaders try many ways to intimidate him, testing him with political situations and made-up scenarios. Like the story they create about seven brothers who all die consecutively after being married to one woman (Matthew 22:23–28). Jesus, however, never cringes in fear or backs away from confronting them.

Even as a twelve-year-old, he could comfortably sit among the teachers of his day. "Three days later they finally discovered him [Jesus] in the Temple, sitting among the religious teachers, listening to them and asking questions" (Luke 2:46).

Throughout his ministry, Jesus continues to ask questions. This shows his courage and willingness to discuss difficult topics. That's possible only in someone secure and happy in their relationship with God.

Jesus never feels obligated to answer a question just because someone asked. Sometimes he answers with another question (Matthew 21:24) or with a story, like the Good Samaritan (Luke 10:30), and lets his listeners work out the correct response.

In Jesus, we see God using questions to patiently draw out the contents of a person's heart. Jesus has no reason to feel threatened or defend himself against those who oppose him. Nor does he beat them into submission or criticize their opinions. Instead, he whets their appetite and encourages them to delve deeper. Jesus's confidence in his relationship with his Father means that difficult subjects, intimidating questions, and the pressure to conform don't steal his joy.

God's Anger

How do we reconcile a happy God with his anger? "God shows his anger from heaven against all sinful, wicked people who suppress the truth by their wickedness" (Romans 1:18).

Speaking about God's anger makes us feel uncomfortable if we associate it with human emotion, like the irritation of a parent whose child disobeys or a boss who's unhappy with an employee. Human anger is often selfish. We become angry when we don't get our own way, when our objectives are blocked, or when we're inconvenienced.

Injustice angers God.

God's anger is selfless. He becomes angry when the poor are oppressed, when the underprivileged are disadvantaged, and when corruption ruins our legal system.

When we look at Jesus's life, we note he directs his anger mostly at the Pharisees. These religious leaders of his day are more interested in maintaining their traditions than showing compassion to the poor, more concerned with rule-keeping than seeking a relationship with God, and more anxious about preserving their status than rejoicing in the healing of the sick.

This is most clearly seen when Jesus healed the man with a shriveled hand on the Sabbath.

> He looked around at them angrily and was deeply saddened by their hard hearts. Then he said to the man, "Hold out your hand." So the man held out his hand, and it was restored! At once the Pharisees went away and met with the supporters of Herod to plot how to kill Jesus. (Mark 3:5–6)

The Pharisees think it's wrong to heal on the Sabbath but okay to plot murder! No wonder Jesus is angry.

God's anger is the natural outworking of his love. The more deeply we love, the more injustice offends us. God is incensed by wickedness, which hurts both the victim and the perpetrator. From the beginning, God has a plan to deal with sin. Through Moses, God institutes the sacrificial system, which teaches that sin can be atoned for only through sacrifice. This is a picture of what God ultimately had in mind. Jesus would serve as the sacrificial Lamb "who takes away the sin of the world!" (John 1:29).

This pictures not an angry God punishing his Son vindictively but rather a loving Father seeking justice and a Son willingly laying down his life to achieve this. "No one can take my life from me. I sacrifice it voluntarily. For I have the authority to lay it down when I want to and also to take it up again" (10:18).

Yes, God's anger is real, but it has been appeased in Jesus.

Yet we still live in a broken world with much suffering and hardship.

The God Perspective

Believing in a happy God while reading daily news reports of violence, crime, and anguish may seem cruel. What was God thinking to create a world with so much suffering?

God is the ultimate big-picture thinker. He sees our pain as short-term because its duration is brief compared to eternity. An exercise regime, an operation, chemotherapy can all cause temporary pain and inconvenience. My husband, Ross, underwent six months of chemotherapy following a cancer diagnosis, but that was thirty years ago. Now I can look back and know the distress of the situation was temporary yet it produced long-term benefits—not only to his health but to our deeper understanding of God. Our short-term pain led to long-term gain. However, our pain doesn't come only from events we can't control but also from bad choices, both our own and those of others.

God knew creating people with free will was deeply problematic.

He knew that people would abuse this outlandish privilege. When we hear of oppression, violence, and bloodshed, we see the evidence of this. Yet, he made plans to deal with the crisis before it even happened. In the short term, he grieves the suffering sin brings to those who perpetrate it and live with its consequences. However, in the long term, justice and restoration are coming.

Good mysteries end with the villains exposed, the heroes exonerated, and justice enforced. Likewise, in the final chapters of the New Testament, we see the forces of evil exposed, Christians exonerated, and justice enforced.

We win!

God's story ends with a wedding feast, a celebration, a happily-ever-after ending. The last page is written. Long-term gain and reward await those who seek it. We can face the pain of this world because we know we will be rewarded for our faith.

> He will wipe every tear from their eyes, and there will be no more death or sorrow or crying or pain. All these things are gone forever.
> And the one sitting on the throne said, "Look, I am making everything new!" (Revelation 21:4–5)

Ultimately, we will see the destruction of evil. In the meantime, we rejoice that through Jesus's death and resurrection, we can be happy now.

Ways to Increase Happiness

History can be compared to an enormous painting. The painting has both light and dark colors, and the overall effect is stunning. People in art galleries don't stand immediately in front of the pictures and focus solely on the dark patches. They don't obsess that a painting is spoiled by the inclusion of shade but rather stand back and admire the overall effect. Likewise, while God isn't oblivious to the darkness of grief and suffering, he's happy with the final outcome.

A new world is coming where there will be no more pain.

Learning to be happy may take some time and be more difficult than we expect. As our relationship with God matures, he renews our minds, transforms our thinking, and changes our attitudes. Happiness isn't an ornament that God will hang on our lives. Rather, it's a fruit that grows as we allow our spiritual roots to extend deeper into the soil of our relationship with God. So if we grow in him, we'll smile more often as we share his happiness.

Here are three thoughts to reflect on as you seek to increase your happiness:

- **Remember God's kingdom is righteousness, peace, and joy.** Focusing on his kingdom reminds us that we're part of God's unseen, unending, and unfathomable sovereignty. Therefore, our concerns are small in comparison. "For the Kingdom of God is not a matter of what we eat or drink, but of living a life of goodness and peace and joy in the Holy Spirit" (Romans 14:17).

- **Choose the "God perspective."** By taking a long-term view, we realize this world isn't all there is and our time here is very brief. Knowing suffering is temporary means we can be happy now. "So we don't look at the troubles we can see now; rather, we fix our gaze on things that cannot be seen. For the things we see now will soon be gone, but the things we cannot see will last forever" (2 Corinthians 4:18).

- **Worship regularly.** Worship takes our attention off ourselves and places it on God's character. The more we know and trust God, the more we will feel deeply secure in our relationship with him. "Worship the Lord with gladness. Come before him, singing with joy" (Psalm 100:2).

Gratitude also increases our joy, and we look at that in the next chapter.

Let's Pray

Thank you, Lord, that you are a happy God. Therefore, I can be happy too.

Thank you, too, that you understand what blocks my joy. Help me to overcome these by adopting your perspective.

Help me to feel your anger over injustice and alleviate the pain where I can.

I pray you will stir up in me the desire to pursue your blessings, not just for my own sake but for the sake of others so they'll know you bless your people. May my joy serve as an attractive witness to others.

As I worship I pray I will turn all my attention toward you. Remind me of your promise that as I draw near to you, you will draw near to me.

Help me to connect more deeply with you so I experience the joy of your presence continually.

In Jesus's name.

Amen.

2

God Surprises

One of the most surprising things that has ever happened to me was returning to live in Corryong in northeast Victoria, Australia. We first moved there in 1989, when Ross was appointed to the position of bank manager. I've always liked small rural towns, and I soon fell in love with this one. I loved the scenery. I loved the weather. More than that, I loved the people. I never wanted to leave. But we left in 1993 so Ross could take up his first ministry appointment at a church in Queensland—a fifteen-hour road trip further north. I never expected to live in Corryong again.

In 2007, we went to Corryong for two weeks to help the local church while they searched for a new minister. After arriving, I went to the library to check my email and met someone I knew—not surprising in a small town. However, this person didn't know that since leaving Corryong fourteen years earlier, I had gained a library qualification and worked in a library at the time. She told me their librarian had resigned effective that day. She then bemoaned the difficulty of finding another qualified librarian.

"Who'd move to Corryong for fifteen hours a week?" she asked.

When I started the job I had at that time, I worked only

a few hours a week. I wanted more hours but wasn't sure how many. I remember wondering how God could answer my prayers when I didn't even know what I wanted. About this time, we went to see a friend who was a financial planner. Based on his figures, I worked out that I wanted to work seventeen hours a week.

So while I found the vacancy at the library interesting, I didn't give it much thought. The next evening, I met a woman who worked at the Neighborhood House, formerly the old bank manager's residence and the house we lived in when we previously resided in the town. This woman helped run community courses. She invited me to visit and look at the changes they had made to the house. I dropped in a couple of days later and met the former librarian, who also just happened to be visiting. The librarian started volunteering information about the library job, which I found decidedly odd because she didn't know me or that I worked in a library. Then she said the job was seventeen hours a week because the hours included an extra two to do the banking and write reports. As soon as she said seventeen hours, I knew I had to apply for the job.

Rather strangely, the position description didn't state the exact number of hours, and I wouldn't have known before I applied if the librarian hadn't offered this information.

I inquired and discovered I needed to apply by the next day. I hadn't intended to take my résumé with me to Corryong since I wasn't planning to apply for a job. However, it was on my computer, which I had with me. I subsequently got the job, and shortly afterward the church asked Ross to serve as the minister.

It surprised me that God would choreograph so many incidents to put me in the right place at the right time to hear the right information. God blessed me by arranging for me to live in Corryong once again.

God wants to surprise us.

His lavish, extravagant, generous care and his intimate involvement in my life astonish me. He surprises me with his attention to detail, his foresight, and his consideration of my individuality.

God's Surprise for David

The way God orchestrates events also surprises King David. David wants to build a temple—a house for God. Instead, God tells David through Nathan the prophet that he would build David's house, meaning he would bless David's offspring and create a dynasty for him. David's son Solomon would build the physical temple. David could feel disappointed that he wouldn't build the temple, but instead, he is surprised by the way God orchestrates events for him.

> Who am I, O Sovereign Lord, and what is my family, that you have brought me this far? And now, Sovereign Lord, in addition to everything else, you speak of giving your servant a lasting dynasty! Do you deal with everyone this way, O Sovereign Lord? (2 Samuel 7:18–19)

I love how David registers his surprise, "Do you deal with everyone this way?"

Has God ever surprised you by arranging the circumstances of your life? Did you wonder if it was normal?

David never forgets where he comes from. He hadn't been in line to become the king. He wasn't even the eldest son, but God had taken him from looking after sheep and anointed him king of his people (1 Samuel 16:1–13). David is amazed that God would bless him like this. He knows this happened only because God had chosen him and arranged all his circumstances, including keeping him safe from Saul, so that he was in the right place at the right time with the right information.

David responds with surprise, and this leads to gratitude.

Are we surprised by God working behind the scenes in our lives? Regardless of our background, God works to draw us deeper into relationship with him and show us his purposes for our lives.

God provides for us in so many ways. He arranged our salvation long before we even knew we needed a Savior, which is amazing in itself. And if this isn't enough, God guides, strengthens, and protects us. He has spoken to us about a future home with him. We deserve none of this, yet God has chosen to lavish us with his many blessings. God is immeasurably good to us, and he will surprise us with his goodness if we pay attention.

**The life of faith is an adventure:
Are we willing to be surprised?**

Unpredictability

When I first started reading the Gospels fifty years ago, I found Jesus surprising and unpredictable. He never responded how I expected, and I was wary of engaging with God when I couldn't predict how he would respond.

These days, I'm more spiritually mature, so I expect to have God all worked out! Yet Jesus still occasionally does something completely outside my understanding. For instance, Jesus heals the man at the pool of Bethesda without the man even knowing who he is. When the healed man is asked why he's carrying his mat on the Sabbath, he says:

> The man who healed me told me, "Pick up your mat and walk."
> "Who said such a thing as that?" they demanded.
> The man didn't know, for Jesus had disappeared into the crowd. (John 5:11–13)

I know God wants us to come to him with our requests. I know God wants us to express our faith in him. I know God wants us to avoid wrong behavior. But then Jesus heals this man when none of these things are true. The man doesn't ask for healing, he doesn't express faith in Jesus since he doesn't even know who he is, and later Jesus tells him to, "stop sinning, or something even worse may happen to you" (v. 14).

When Jesus asks him if he wants to be well, I'm

expecting an enthusiastic "Yes, I do." Instead, he comes up with an excuse. "I have no one to put me into the pool when the water bubbles up. Someone else always gets there ahead of me" (v. 7).

His response makes me wonder if he has become comfortable with his lot in life and isn't interested in Jesus interrupting his circumstances by making him well. All of which causes me to wonder why Jesus picks this man out of the crowd to be healed.

Lots of people lie by the pool, why doesn't Jesus heal someone more deserving?

I'm tempted to reduce my relationship with God to a formula.

My formula says if I behave in a certain way, pray using certain words, or use sufficient volume, then God must answer my prayer. But no, God is never obligated to me. We fall into the trap of wanting a standard operating procedure for God's responses because this would be less challenging than having an honest relationship with him. Anytime I think God is swayed by my ingenuity or by my vocabulary, I'm not operating out of relationship. God is surprising and doesn't function according to a blueprint.

Even Jesus expresses surprise.

A Roman centurion sends some Jewish elders, who plead earnestly with Jesus to come and heal the centurion's servant, who is nearing death. The Jewish elders think very highly of this centurion (which is a surprise in itself since he's part of the nation that oppresses Israel). They speak on his behalf, "'If anyone deserves your help, he does,' they said, 'for he loves the Jewish people and even built a synagogue for us'" (Luke 7:4–5).

Perhaps the centurion doesn't think Jesus will come, because when he finds out that he's on his way, he sends some friends to tell Jesus that he doesn't deserve to have him come to his house. The centurion probably realizes the Jews will consider Jesus unclean if he enters a gentile home (Acts 10:28). Instead, the centurion gives Jesus this message: "Just say the word from where you are, and my servant will be healed" (Luke 7:7).

Jesus then marvels at the faith of the Roman centurion (v. 9). Jesus doesn't expect a gentile to have more faith than a Jew.

The other time Jesus is surprised occurs in his hometown. Sadly, it's a lack of faith by his relatives and neighbors that surprises him (Mark 6:6). He expects more from those who know him well.

Sometimes, we may think that when Jesus was on earth, he knew everything and nothing would surprise him, but that wasn't the case. Jesus truly "gave up his divine privileges ... He humbled himself in obedience to God and died a criminal's death on a cross" (Philippians 2:7–8).

Likewise, we often don't know what God has in mind. Our journey of faith will take us in directions that will surprise us, and we may not know in advance how our circumstances will turn out.

More Surprises

In many ways, the most surprising event during Jesus's time on earth is when he turns water into wine at a wedding. Mary reports to Jesus that the hosts have run out of wine, but Jesus isn't motivated to act. Not knowing what God will do, he says to his mother, "My time has not yet come" (John 2:4).

Yet Mary instructs the servants to "do whatever he tells you" (v. 5). This becomes Jesus's first miracle, so Mary has no historical grounds to believe Jesus will do something supernatural. Yet, she knows her son is kind, so perhaps she thinks he might do something. But who would've predicted turning water into wine?

Jesus's response is totally out of proportion to the need. Running out of wine at a wedding is a major social embarrassment, but surely not serious enough to warrant a miracle. Jesus doesn't perform his first miracle to save someone from dying or to heal an incurable disease. That would come later. For his first miracle, he turns the water in six large jars into wine. Each jar contains about 25 gallons[1]—an enormous quantity. And it isn't ordinary wine. It's good quality wine wasted on guests who've already had enough to drink (v. 10). The quantity and quality of the wine speak of God's abundant provision.

Peter, also called Simon, has a similar experience. One day after Jesus finishes preaching, he says to Peter, "Now go out where it is deeper, and let down your nets to catch some fish" (Luke 5:4).

The resulting catch is so large that it nearly sinks two boats (v. 7).

Another time Jesus feeds five thousand people and even produces leftovers. "So they picked up the pieces and filled twelve baskets with scraps left by the people who had eaten from the five barley loaves" (John 6:13).

Again, God provides more than enough. What if God surprises us by giving us more than we ask for?

God doesn't just want to meet our needs. He wants to provide more than enough.

Often when we pray, we have limited outcomes in mind. We have expectations and would prefer God solve our problems quickly and quietly, but what if God wants to do something surprising? Something entirely different from our expectations? Are we open to that? When we overcome any hesitancy on our part and fully trust the outcome to Jesus, we open the way for God's abundant provision.

Paying Attention

Recently, I was listening to Matt Redman's song "Once Again." Redman's wonder of God's goodness toward us struck me, and it made me wonder too. Every day, we have the opportunity to consider God's graciousness to us and be surprised.

I've heard the story of Jesus's sacrificial death and his resurrection many, many times. How do I avoid taking God's goodness for granted?

On Jesus's last night with his disciples, he tells them to remember (Luke 22:19). As I remember, I deliberately focus on Jesus's death and the agony he suffered on the cross. I reflect on the massive price God paid to forgive me. I consider the extravagant gift of God's mercy, and I begin to recognize how surprising it is that God would take responsibility to deal with my sin.

Are we staggered at the magnitude of the sacrifice God made for us? Are we overwhelmed by the mercy of God?

God's mercy transforms us in a way punishment and

reprimands never do. Punishments are often an ineffective way of changing behavior. So many criminals reoffend, the same children get into trouble at school, and parents repeat the same rebukes to their offspring.

Yet, when I realize that I'm the recipient of the most undeserved mercy and grace, I'm amazed, humbled, and changed on the inside. When David experiences God's forgiveness following the incident with Bathsheba, he wants to be different: "Create in me a clean heart, O God. Renew a loyal spirit within me" (Psalm 51:10).

This is the effect God hopes mercy will have on us—a desire to change. When we read the history of God's people, particularly in the Old Testament, we find they often take God's mercy for granted with little thought to its enormity or value.

Taken for Granted

Likewise, in modern Western society, we take much for granted. Few things pleasantly surprise us and gratitude for simply being alive is often absent. For example, giving and receiving gifts has become so commercialized and so expected that we've lost our sense of surprise, and then we lost our gratitude. Giving has become a reciprocating arrangement that doesn't move us. Our response to a thoughtful gift ought to be surprise that someone would be so kind and an appreciative attitude for their thoughtfulness.

Too often I'm like the students who R. C. Sproul writes about in *The Holiness of God*. During his time as a university lecturer, Sproul granted two extensions of time on two different assignments. Afterward, he discovered that the students came to expect that they would always be given more time to complete the work. They were no longer surprised by his kindness. Instead, they took it for granted. Even worse, they considered it unfair if he refused to give them more time.[2]

If we don't take the time to reflect on someone's kindness toward us, feelings of entitlement can sneak up on us.

Gratitude acknowledges that we're in someone's debt. Sometimes people will express their thanks by saying "much obliged" or "I owe you." This communicates their sense of indebtedness. When we feel indebted, we may also feel dependent on someone else's efforts. Perhaps this explains why we don't always feel a sense of gratitude. We may not want to acknowledge our indebtedness, our inadequacies, or our need for help. We would rather believe that we're self-sufficient and capable of handling whatever life throws at us.

Our friend, incapacitated with a bad back, refused to have visitors. The only person he would let help him was his wife. She was the only one he would allow to see his helplessness. I wondered what it would look like for this man if he had allowed others to surprise him with their kindness. Would he have been able to express his gratitude? Or would he have sought to repay them?

Surprise Stealers

What prevents us from being surprised?

We stop being surprised when we forget God's blessings and focus on our difficulties. The Israelites, who see God drown their Egyptian oppressors, quickly forget God's miraculous intervention and soon turn to grumbling and complaining. The outcomes aren't good (Numbers 14:1–3; 16:1–42; 21:4–9).

When I whine, I accuse God of not looking after me the way I want, of keeping good things from me, or of not knowing what's best for me. When I find fault, I say God isn't good. God has given me so much. But when I complain, I say it's not enough and I want more.

God hates it when I gripe.

I complain when I forget to pay attention to God's goodness. I forget to celebrate my salvation, my freedom from my past, and my hope for the future. I take God for granted and am no longer surprised.

Complaining has nothing to do with money, power, or intelligence. Instead, it reflects our attitude toward our circumstances. As Christians, we know, whatever our circumstances, God is in control, and, therefore, we can accept whatever happens as ultimately beneficial.

However, it's not easy. One of our pastoral moves meant living in a church house that was quite old, inadequately heated, and not well maintained. To make matters worse, we had moved out of our own modern house to accept the position. Yet, I knew God wanted us to minister in this church. It was hard not to focus on what I missed and instead pay attention to the many blessings I still experienced.

> Do everything without complaining and arguing, so that no one can criticize you.

> Live clean, innocent lives as children of God, shining like bright lights in a world full of crooked and perverse people. (Philippians 2:14–15)

This verse gives us another compelling reason not to complain. If we don't complain, it will be obvious to those around us that we're Christians. We will stand out like stars in the night sky.

Isn't it surprising to think we can have such a big impact by simply not complaining?

Paul learns "the secret of being content in any and every situation, whether well fed or hungry, whether living in plenty or in want" (Philippians 4:12 NIV), and he does it by thinking about what's "true, and honorable, and right, and pure, and lovely, and admirable" (v. 8).

Paul shows us that the secret to contentment, and therefore avoiding the temptation to complain, is learning to pay attention to what we think about.

Disappointment

Another surprise stealer is the disappointment that comes from dissatisfaction. John Piper, Bible college lecturer and pastor, said, "God is most glorified in us when we're most satisfied in him."[3] This is a surprising thought. We glorify God by being satisfied. We tend to think we glorify God most when we're busy working for him. However, when we're satisfied with him as our heavenly Father, content to be his child, and happy for him to arrange the circumstances of our lives, we demonstrate our faith in his provision.

Finding satisfaction in God takes faith, and this glorifies him.

Sadly, at times, I wasn't satisfied with God. Sometimes I felt disappointed with the way God made me. I've wished for a louder voice and one that would always sing in tune. I've wished for a more extroverted personality. When I think like this, I accuse God of doing a bad job. I accuse him of not knowing what he was doing when he made me because I'm not satisfied with his work. The truth is, God did know and he planned and purposed my particular mix of gifts, abilities, and personality.

Others are dissatisfied with various aspects of their appearance. Those with curly hair wish for straight hair, those with straight hair wish for curly hair, and some would just be grateful for hair. Some think their nose, mouth, or feet are too big or too small, or maybe they wish they were shorter, smarter, or more sprightly.

Sometimes, we don't find our job or our marriage partner satisfying. Perhaps going to a different school, living in a different town, or marrying someone else would have improved our lives. Others seem to have it easier. Life is a struggle. Things work out better for other people. We feel disappointed that God doesn't bless us more so our lives would run more smoothly.

The remedy is to redirect our thoughts and focus on the blessings we have in Christ. We will not only learn to be satisfied but also open the way for God to surprise us.

God has many surprises in store for us, and they will come unexpectedly, like a refreshing summer shower.

They remind us God is there, he cares, and he wants to be involved in our lives. Surprises teach us not only gratitude but also childlike trust in anticipation of the good things God wants to give us. He gives us hope, happiness, security, purpose, eternal life—and so much more.

Will we accept the invitation and pay attention to the God who surprises?

Let's Pray

Thank you, Lord, that you surprise me with your goodness and give me so many reasons to be grateful. You are immeasurably good to me, yet so often I take you for granted. Give me fresh eyes to see your many blessings in my life, and may others see these in my life too.

Help me, Lord, to be open to all that you want to do in my life, church, and community. Empower me to be brave and give you the freedom to answer my prayers with your abundance, even when it requires me to stretch spiritually as I go through new experiences.

Convict me when I am tempted to complain and remind me that I am indeed blessed. Help me to pay attention to the many ways you touch my life.

In Jesus's name.

Amen.

3

God Frees

"Keep short accounts with God," I was told as a young Christian. Apparently, every night before I go to sleep, I ought to confess all the sins I've committed that day to God. This struck me as odd. But I didn't grow up in a Christian environment, and my Christian friends seemed to agree, so I accepted it. But it created a picture in my mind of God as a heavenly Accountant with a red pen ticking off my debts.

What if I missed one and didn't confess all my sins?

Some sins aren't single acts and are therefore harder to itemize, for example, unbelief, improper thinking, and inappropriate attitudes. I also struggled with "sins of omission"—lack of love, lack of tolerance, lack of faith. Merely confessing them didn't change anything.

I also couldn't imagine why God would want to hear recitations of everyone's shortcomings. It wasn't like God didn't know. I found the exercise tedious.

"God, am I boring you?"

Then, one day I heard a life-changing sermon titled "Up-to-the-Minute Forgiveness."[1] I learned I could live guilt-free. God isn't the stingy accountant, meting out his grace sin by sin. His grace abounds like an ocean. I don't have to worry that I might die with unconfessed sin in my life because his grace covers all my sins.

He lavishes us with his grace, so we can live guilt-free.

We can live secure in the knowledge that his supply of grace suffices for all our sins—past, present, and future. God gives his grace with abandon, richly, freely, and plentifully. He has a bottomless supply made available to us through the death and resurrection of his Son. This grace is pure gift. We never have to lift a finger to earn it, and it's always accessible. He's ridiculously generous with his grace (Matthew 20:1–15). But do we avail ourselves of it?

Up-to-the-Minute Forgiveness

What is up-to-the-minute forgiveness?

John teaches us, "If we are living in the light, as God is in the light, then we have fellowship with each other, and the blood of Jesus, his Son, cleanses us from all sin" (1 John 1:7). If we've committed our lives to God, then we've committed ourselves to live in the light. John doesn't mention keeping a list of sins to confess. Jesus's blood provides a continuous purification from sin as we live out our Christian walk.

The animal sacrifices in the Old Testament could not atone for sin. "But instead, those sacrifices actually reminded them of their sins year after year" (Hebrews 10:3). God always knew this, of course, but he sought to teach his people an important truth. Anything we sacrifice is never enough to relieve us of guilt. We need a Savior.

God doesn't want us to constantly remember our sins. Through Jesus's death and resurrection, he would release us from our sins so we can live without a guilty conscience (v. 22). God abundantly provides for us so we can live in a constant state of forgiveness and experience freedom from guilt.

God deals so completely with our sins that he calls us "saints." These days, the word *saint* refers to someone a church has officially recognized for their holiness or their self-sacrifice and hard work. The New Testament authors don't use the word *saint* this way. Paul typically addresses his letters to the "saints" in a certain city. "To the saints who are in Ephesus, and faithful in Christ Jesus" (Ephesians 1:1 NKJV). "To all the saints in Christ Jesus who are in Philippi" (Philippians 1:1 NKJV). Paul understands that all Christians are saints—not because we've achieved some high standard of holiness but because God achieved it for us.

We are saints.

However, we're often reluctant to call ourselves saints because we don't feel holy. Fortunately, God's truth doesn't depend on our feelings, so we can still accept how God sees us. God's true perspective allows us to dispute the devil's lies when he reminds us of our failings and tries to make us feel unworthy.

Being saints doesn't mean we never confess our sins to God. Certainly, if we feel God convicting us about something we've done or left undone, we confess and repent. Nevertheless, God has freed us from the necessity of keeping track of our sins. Paul says love "keeps no record of being wronged" (1 Corinthians 13:5). Likewise, God keeps no record of our wrongdoing. God has dealt with sin so completely that we can live free from the worry of past sins and the anxiety of future failings.

As a child, I went to Australian rules football matches. In this form of football, a player can continue pursuing the ball even if they drop it or a player has fumbled the ball in a contest. In this scenario, God is like the umpire calling out, "Play on, play on," while we lie in the dust, bemoaning the fact we dropped the ball. Yes, we fail, but when we do, we confess it to God, get up, and play on.

But "playing on" doesn't mean trying harder.

Freedom Stealers

Sometimes I make New Year's resolutions to eat healthily, exercise more, and find a perfect way of organizing my bookshelves, while simultaneously quitting my perfectionism! Like most people, I struggle to keep resolutions. Paul explains the reason for our failure. "I know that nothing good lives in me, that is, in my sinful nature. I want to do what is right, but I can't" (Romans 7:18).

Paul goes on to thank God for rescuing him from trying harder to change his behavior (v. 25). The compulsion to try harder to live a godly life is a freedom stealer. God desires to liberate us by providing his enabling grace.

Outside of Christian faith, grace is rarely experienced. I grew up hearing there's no such thing as a free lunch. So when I learned God offers his grace freely, I was suspicious. What does God really want in return? I knew God is a holy God, so I concluded he wanted me to live a holy life. I tried to be more loving, patient, and forgiving. When I failed, I tried harder, but my self-initiated self-improvement programs had limited success.

Paul writes to the Galatians, "After starting your new lives in the Spirit, why are you now trying to become perfect by your own human effort?" (Galatians 3:3).

What changed my behavior in the first place was focusing on what Christ has done for me, not concentrating on my own efforts. I'm to continue my Christian walk the same way as I started, by remembering it's Jesus who did the work. On the cross, he declared, "It is finished!" (John 19:30). He completed the work of salvation, and now as I reflect on all God has done for me, I discover I can rest in Christ's finished work and allow him to make the necessary changes in my life. "And the Lord—who is the Spirit—makes us more and more like him as we are changed into his glorious image" (2 Corinthians 3:18).

Jesus changes us by his Spirit, not by us trying to give ourselves an upgrade.

The more we open our lives up to receive his grace, the more he changes us.

Another Freedom Stealer

Over the centuries, God inspired people to put together a book, the Bible. He didn't intend it as a rule book. Indeed, it tells stories of how God intervened in people's lives. Nevertheless, our human nature would rather have a rule book. We'd rather follow a set of rules than seek God's direction. Reading the Bible to make sure we follow the rules is another freedom stealer.

When the Galatians find that submitting to Jewish law results in less persecution than standing firm in the freedom God has given them, they succumb to rule keeping. But Paul rebukes them, "Oh, foolish Galatians!" (Galatians 3:1).

Before this outburst, Paul explains, "If keeping the law could make us right with God, then there was no need for Christ to die" (2:21).

Similarly, Paul writes to the church in Rome explaining how God credited Abraham with righteousness because of faith, not because of his heritage, good works, or obedience.

> And when God counted him as righteous, it wasn't just for Abraham's benefit. It was recorded for our benefit, too, assuring us that God will also count us as righteous if we believe in him, the one who raised Jesus our Lord from the dead. (Romans 4:23–24)

God not only forgives but also credits us with righteousness. God's extravagant grace means we're better off now, than if we'd never sinned. We're given righteousness, something we've never had before and can't earn.

Some mistakenly think that people in Old Testament times obtain righteousness by making animal sacrifices and keeping the law, but this isn't the case. People in the

Old Testament are also justified by faith—Abel, Enoch, Noah, Joseph, Moses, and many others are people of faith (Hebrews 11).

The only type of righteousness in the entire Bible is righteousness by faith.

In the Old Testament, people keep the law as evidence of the faith they already have. And if they don't keep the law, it shows their lack of faith because it means they don't trust God's ways. "This Good News tells us how God makes us right in his sight. This is accomplished from start to finish by faith. As the Scriptures say, 'It is through faith that a righteous person has life'" (Romans 1:17).

Believing we're saved by faith alone is relatively easy when we avoid obvious sin. But what about those times when we fail and do the wrong thing?

Then it takes genuine faith to believe and confess the truth: that we're just as righteous as we were before we fell into that sin.

Righteousness is a gift, and we don't lose the gift if we sin. Live in this truth.

The Point of the Law

This leads to the question, "Why, then, was the law given?" (Galatians 3:19).

Indeed, if we can't keep the law, why give it to us? When God gave the Ten Commandments, he knew we'd never be able to keep them unless we relied on him.

The commandments don't benefit God. They benefit us by helping us recognize our need for a Savior. We can't possibly hope to meet God's standards by our own efforts. Never could, never will. The purpose of the law is to guide us to Christ and faith in him (v. 24).

The more I read Galatians, the more aware I become that it's Paul's most dangerous letter. Paul advocates so much freedom it's scary. "And now that the way of faith has come, we no longer need the law as our guardian" (v. 25).

If we're no longer under a guardian—a supervisor of the law—then there are no rules, and we're truly free to do whatever we choose.

As a parent, would you give this much freedom to your child? Would you tell your children they're free to do whatever they like?

I had consistent bedtimes for my children and expectations around mealtimes. Consequently, my children arrived at church on a Sunday morning fed and well rested. This meant they were full of energy and looking for action. Sitting still and being quiet wasn't on their agenda. Other parents, I noticed, let their children go to bed and eat whenever they felt like it. Their children arrived at church happy to snooze or eat. Some days, I wondered about the value of my rules!

Nevertheless, giving children no rules at all would be seriously scary. Young children find security in rules, but, as God's children, God expects us to be mature enough not to need them. But this is scary for adults too. What would people do without rules?

Church leadership may try to control attendees' behavior by creating guidelines, such as don't go to dodgy movies, don't date nonchurchgoers, and don't drink. While it's good and proper to teach people to act responsibly, we have to be careful that our guidelines don't become rules.

**Creating rules for good behavior
doesn't promote God's cause.**

Missing the Point

The Pharisees think they promote God's cause by enforcing a lot of regulations not found in their Hebrew Scriptures, but they miss the point—righteousness comes by faith.

How could they miss it? These people are Jews and have known the Scriptures all their lives.

> Because instead of trusting God, *they* took over. They were absorbed in what they themselves were doing. They were so absorbed in their "God projects" that they didn't notice God right in front of them. (Romans 9:31–32 MSG)

I know how easily I become absorbed in my "God projects." A while ago, I organized a Christian Writers' Conference. I became so busy I neglected God's call on my life to write. Creating registration forms and spreadsheets of attendees is less challenging than writing from my heart about my spiritual journey. Trivial tasks easily sidetracked me during my most productive writing time.

It's not only the bad things in life that keep us from God's best. Quite often it's the good.

Living by faith is challenging. God is indeed right there

in front of me, loving me, encouraging me, convicting me. But sometimes it's all too overwhelming, and I fall back into the habit of wanting some clear-cut rules.

Man-Made Rules

Paul writes about the deceitfulness of man-made rules. They have the appearance of wisdom. They give us a sense of security and appear to be spiritual. They offer a way of measuring success, which appears beneficial. They help us feel responsible, but they lack any value when it comes to lasting change in our behavior (Colossians 2:16–23).

Rule keeping has negatively impacted my life. The times I've managed to do what I perceive is good, I've become proud and self-righteous. But when I've failed to do what I perceive is good, I've felt condemned and disqualified. Neither outcome is what God intends. Over time, I learned to place my priorities where God places them—not on an outward adherence to standards of behavior that have the appearance of wisdom but rather on a heart relationship with Jesus.

Besides, Jesus breaks the rules.

He touches lepers, forgives adulterers, and "works" on the Sabbath (Matthew 8:3; John 8:1–11; Mark 3:1–6). Jesus knows God's heart, so he knows when and where it's appropriate to break the rules. His concern for people and his dependency on his Father guide him.

Peter breaks the rules when he enters a gentile home. He does this with great reluctance and only after receiving a vision from God (Acts 10).

Rahab breaks the rules and tells a lie. However, her actions, based on faith, are credited to her as righteousness

(Joshua 2:5–6; Hebrews 11:31).

The law has a purpose, not to keep us worried about whether or not we do the right thing but rather to lead us to Christ. But so often the law has been used to drive people away. Some have been driven away because they have a child born outside of marriage, have been through a divorce, have an addiction, or have unusual fashion choices. Likewise, there've been times—many times—when I felt like I could never measure up, like I had failed too badly and was too tired to try anymore. As a young Christian, I had high expectations of myself. I thought I should be able to maintain a disciplined lifestyle of spending time every day reading the Bible, praying regularly for everyone I knew, and keeping my thought life in check. Instead, I failed to meet my own self-imposed rules.

The law is intended to lead us into the freedom of a relationship like Jesus had with his Father so that we're doing the will of God from our hearts (Ephesians 6:6).

Yes-No Answers

The Pharisees don't understand that God wants his people to do his will from their hearts. They come to Jesus with their moral or ethical dilemmas, wanting a ruling. For example, "Is it right to pay taxes to Caesar or not?" They expect a yes-no answer. Instead, Jesus says to them, "Give to Caesar what belongs to Caesar, and give to God what belongs to God" (Mark 12:14, 17).

Jesus gives them a principle and lets them work out the details for themselves. God often works this way. I would prefer yes-no answers. Is it right to watch this movie? Can

I attend this event? Am I allowed to skip church today? In these situations, God rarely gives yes-no answers because he has already given principles, and he expects me to think through how to apply them. These principles are found throughout the Bible. For example, "it is more blessed to give than to receive" (Acts 20:35). And "do to others as you would like them do to you" (Luke 6:31).

God knows giving us a principle rather than a yes-no answer will cause conflict because Christians will come to different conclusions as to what is acceptable behavior.

In your life, who defines acceptable behavior?

God doesn't want robots who obey orders without thinking. He wants friends (John 15:15) who will pray things through with him. As believers mature, we're better equipped to handle situations where a new believer may struggle or fall into temptation. Therefore, God may send one believer into a sleazy hotel to be his witness, whereas he may deter another believer from going to the exact same venue.

Consequently, we can't insist other believers adhere to our conscience on these issues. Our responsibility is to spend time praying through what God says to us. God gives us enormous freedom and privilege but also the responsibility to make our decisions based on pleasing our Father.

Seems Good

Even in the early church, decisions aren't made according to clear-cut rules.

The early church has to grapple with the particular issue of how to include believing gentiles in Christian activities.

Should they be circumcised? Should they be required to keep the Sabbath? This is a monumental decision. It would determine the entire future direction of the church. After much discussion, all they say is "it seemed good to the Holy Spirit and to us...." (Acts 15:28).

Surely, this would be the time for something concrete from God—a confirming sign, a prophecy, or handwriting on the wall. Instead, all they receive is a sense that "it seemed good." And what "seemed good"? "You must abstain from eating food offered to idols, from consuming blood or the meat of strangled animals, and from sexual immorality" (v. 29).

Even these requirements aren't binding. "If you do this, you will do well" (v. 29). However, the requirements promote unity between believing gentiles and Jews.[2] These early church leaders make the decision based on the judgment "we should not make it difficult for the Gentiles who are turning to God" (v. 19).

Do our expectations make it difficult for those coming to faith?

Some time ago I heard about a church that wanted to reach out to drug addicts in their area. However, the long-standing members expected these addicts to be free from their addictions before they would welcome them into their worship services. Sadly, these new people stopped coming. If we want to see people come to faith, we can't wait until they live godly lifestyles. People will come with their problems, and the way we respond will have a significant impact on their spiritual growth.

God gives us the freedom to discern his will in our situations. He provides us with his Spirit and the "peace that comes from Christ" to "rule in [our] hearts"

(Colossians 3:15).

God's Spirit and his peace guide us, and it's enough.

Enough? That's so enigmatic. Nevertheless, if God's Spirit has cleansed and renewed our hearts, then he's able to guide and direct us in godly ways. Then, we too can say that the decisions we make seem "good to the Holy Spirit and to us."

Out of Reverence

Nehemiah has a simple standard of behavior. "But out of reverence for God I did not act like that" (Nehemiah 5:15 NIV).

No long-winded lists, no legalistic attitude, but a sincere reverence for God. In this way, Nehemiah pleases God out of a sense of gratitude and freedom, not obligation. We may have different ideas about what constitutes "reverence for God," and these ideas may vary from culture to culture, but God looks at our heart attitude, our motivation.

God is more interested in *why* we do something than in *what* we do.

Therefore, we devote our efforts to becoming more sensitive to God's Spirit within us. This is a harder task. I can't simply copy someone else's standards. This is an ongoing challenge as I grow in my relationship with God.

I am amazed that God allows us so much freedom. My

responsibility is to continually receive the grace that I've found in God and allow it to teach me to act in reverence for him (Titus 2:11–12 NIV). God's grace will motivate and enable me to avoid those things that displease him.

Receiving his grace humbles me. I realize I'm inadequate to live a godly life by my efforts. However, over time, the discomfort of receiving grace becomes like the discomfort of a new pair of shoes. The more I walk in God's grace, the more natural it becomes.

Let's Pray

Thank you, Lord, for providing a way for me to live a guilt-free life. The death and resurrection of your Son means you have completely dealt with my sins, past, present, and future. I am so grateful to be free from my sins and continually cleansed as I walk with you.

Thank you, Lord, for your truly amazing grace. Help me open my heart to receive it and not fall for the freedom stealers of trying harder and rule-keeping.

I pray I will become more sensitive to your Holy Spirit and grow in my understanding of what pleases you so I can make decisions based on reverence for you and on what seems good to the Holy Spirit.

In Jesus's Name.
Amen.

4.

God Identifies with Us

I like to watch murder mysteries—as long as they aren't too gruesome and can be solved in an hour. (Wouldn't it be nice if all of life's mysteries could be resolved in one hour?) Crime mysteries are often fleshed out around the motive. Every detail of the victim's life is investigated. A plot twist occurs, a motive appears, and everything becomes clear. With the criminal captured and the mystery solved, we're satisfied.

Christian faith contains a great mystery.

"Without question, this is the great mystery of our faith: Christ was revealed in a human body" (1 Timothy 3:16).

This is a plot twist the Jews don't expect. The thought of God coming in a human body hasn't occurred to them. Yes, they anticipate a Messiah. But they expect a fully grown Messiah, a compelling, conquering champion, not one who shows compassion to the oppressed, challenges their traditions, and sacrifices his life for their offenses.

This is a great mystery. God chooses to take on flesh, but not because he's short on options. He could shout to us from heaven, write his decrees in the sky, send a superhero, an alien, or thousands upon thousands of angels. He could send a fully grown Messiah to the wilderness to meet with John the Baptist and begin his ministry from there. After all, some erroneously believe that "when the Messiah comes, he will simply appear; no one will know where he comes from" (John 7:27). More understandably, he could disown us and start over again in another galaxy. Instead, he comes as a helpless baby.

God identifies with us by becoming a fully human, ordinary person.

God cares enough to leave the splendor of heaven to enter our mundane world. Jesus brings us face-to-face with a God who not only declares his interest in his creation but also demonstrates his intense desire to connect with us.

But will we connect with this God who knows us intimately?

Jesus's Earthly Life

Jesus experiences a normal Jewish upbringing, and it's not obvious he's the Messiah. John the Baptist doesn't realize that Jesus is the Messiah until God reveals it.

> I saw the Holy Spirit descending like a dove from heaven and resting upon him. I didn't know he was the one, but when God sent me to baptize with water, he told me, "The one on whom you see the Spirit descend and rest is the one who will baptize with the Holy Spirit." I saw this happen to Jesus, so I testify that he is the Chosen One of God. (John 1:32–34)

Jesus's brothers also don't notice anything special about Jesus and aren't supportive of his ministry.

> One time Jesus entered a house, and the crowds began to gather again. Soon he and his disciples couldn't even find time to eat. When his family heard what was happening, they tried to take him away. "He's out of his mind," they said. (Mark 3:20–21)

Even his mother feels the need to have a private chat with him (v. 31).

On another occasion, when it's time for the Jewish Festival of Shelters, his brothers say to him, "'Leave here and go to Judea, where your followers can see your miracles! You can't become famous if you hide like this! If you can do such wonderful things, show yourself to the world!' For even his brothers didn't believe in him" (John 7:3–5).

It's easy to underestimate the difficulties of Jesus's home life. He experiences daily life in a regular family, but he's also subject to a lack of understanding and support from those nearest and dearest. Yet Jesus chooses to maintain contact with his family. He doesn't distance himself from them, which he could do as Capernaum becomes his home and the base for his ministry (Matthew 4:13; Mark 2:1).

Jesus would escape these family tensions if God sent him to earth as a fully grown Messiah. Yet, in God's grand plan, Jesus needs to experience all of life—childhood, adolescence, and adulthood. "Because God's children are human beings—made of flesh and blood—the Son also became flesh and blood" (Hebrews 2:14). For Jesus to be "our merciful and faithful High Priest before God" he had to be like us, "in every respect" (v. 17).

Empathy

During his preaching ministry, Rev. Billy Graham told a story about a walk with his sons when they accidentally stepped on an anthill. One of his sons said, "Wouldn't it be wonderful if we could go down and help those ants rebuild their little house that we destroyed?"

Graham said, "It would, but we're too big and they're too little! We couldn't communicate with them."

Graham then took the opportunity to draw an analogy and teach his children a spiritual lesson. He explained that from God's perspective, people are like ants. For God to communicate with us and to show us how to build our lives, he would need to become a human being. This is exactly what he does. God becomes a man.[1]

God could give us a book that starts with the Ten Commandments and continues with good theology and ethics. But Jesus doesn't come to tell us to live a godly life. Rather he comes to exemplify what a godly life looks like.

The book of Isaiah records the prophet's prayer. "Oh, that you would rend the heavens and come down!" (Isaiah 64:1 NIV). The cry of Isaiah's heart is that God would come to earth. Isaiah's task is daunting, to preach God's word to unresponsive people (6:9–10). It's no wonder he wants God to show up. In Jesus, God not only comes down but also stays. He stays by the presence of his Holy Spirit in his people.

When Jesus dies, "the curtain in the sanctuary of the

Temple was torn in two, from top to bottom" (Mark 15:38). This one brief sentence describes an amazing event. No human hand could tear the ornate curtain from the top to the bottom. The torn curtain symbolizes God rending the heavens as he comes down and opens the way for us to enter his presence (Hebrews 10:20–22). What an extraordinary act that shows God's overwhelming desire to be with his people. God wants to deal with anything that stands between me and him, my sin, my shortcomings, my apathy. And he will tear heaven in two to do it. What an awesome thought that the God who made the universe would desire my fellowship that much.

God tears heaven in two to be with us.

Jesus's incarnation takes God's empathy to a practical level. His understanding is based not on his all-knowing nature as Creator but on his experience as a human being. A potter can make a jug and know everything about it, but he wouldn't know how it feels to be a jug.

When Jesus "made himself nothing" (Philippians 2:7 NIV), he set aside all his divine attributes to become human. Therefore he can sympathize with our weaknesses because he is just like us. He understands not only how we feel but why we feel the way we do. He has the resources and empathy to help us in our time of need.

God's personal knowledge of me continues to impact my Christian journey. God knows my heart and thoughts, so he's not surprised by any idea, any temptation, or any sin that might harass me.

Our Identity Can't Be Stolen

Jesus's life, death, and resurrection open the way for us to become the people of God and part of his family. "For you are a chosen people. You are royal priests, a holy nation, God's very own possession. ... Once you had no identity as a people; now you are God's people" (1 Peter 2:9–10).

Before we come to faith, Jesus sees us as orphans (John 14:18). Though we have natural parents, we didn't have a true sense of who we were. Now that we belong to him, God calls us his own. He makes us his children. We gain a sense of belonging and worth because we are his. John writes that we're children of God, and then he emphasizes this: "that is what we are!" (1 John 3:1). Jesus becoming one of us means he can include us in his family.

When the prodigal son packs up his things, takes his inheritance, and leaves, he's still his father's son. When he spends all his money on wild living and sits starving in a pig pen, he's still his father's son. This is why when he comes to his senses, he can go home (Luke 15:13–18). Likewise, as God's children, we can always come home to God. He promises he won't disown us. We can live securely in the knowledge of our identity as children of God.

> **It's important to see ourselves in the same way God sees us.**

We won't act like God's child if we don't think we are. Through God's Word, we have the authority to dispute the devil's lies and remind him that we are indeed God's children. The devil is the father of lies, and his power is in the lie. If we believe the lie, we're controlled by it. If we believe we are a sinner, we will act like a sinner. If we believe we are a child of God, we will act like a child of God.

All sorts of lies drop into our minds. The devil can't steal our identity, but he tempts us to doubt it so that we lose the close sense of fellowship with our heavenly Father. The devil's lies try to convince us we're unlovable, unacceptable, or unworthy of God's attention. He's quick to remind us of our failings. One of his common lies tells us that we are different from other people. That other people are more gifted and more valuable to God, that we've missed our opportunities, or that it's too late to change. These are all lies. Yet, it's our choice whether we believe God's truth or the devil's lies.

When we rebuke the lie and repent of believing it, its power is broken, and we're free to experience the assurance of God's presence.

Up Close and Personal

While Jesus coming to earth means he's deeply connected to us, it also means his messages can get a bit too insightful and a bit too personal. Sometimes, we overlook this since the stories in the New Testament have become so familiar. We disregard their challenging and pointed nature. When Jesus tells stories, he deliberately chooses everyday situations that his listeners would easily relate to. But often he uses images that may distress his hearers. A Jewish boy demanding his inheritance, a Jewish boy in a pigpen, and a Jewish father running (Luke 15) are all abhorrent to a Jew.[2] Jesus intends for his stories to surprise his hearers and to confront them with God's nature, his nearness, and his deep interest in their lives.

For example, we know the story of the good Samaritan (Luke 10:30–37) so well we can miss how barbed it is. When Jesus says "Go and do the same," traditionally we take it to mean we have to help those in need, especially people like Samaritans, who aren't well liked. That's a really good message, which Jesus did teach, but it's not the point of this particular story.

To read this passage as an encouragement to help those who aren't well liked would be to read it as if the man who's robbed and beaten is the despised Samaritan and the man who helps is just like you or me.

The problem is, as Mark Buchanan points out, that's not how Jesus tells the story.[3] The just-like-us person is beaten up and in need of assistance. The despised Samaritan is the one offering help.

When Jesus asks "Which of these three would you say was a neighbor to the man who was attacked by bandits?" (v. 36), the expert in the law receives more than he bargained for. If he'd been alert, he would've said, "Wait a minute, that isn't the question I asked. I want to know who is *my* neighbor? Who is the neighbor of a respectable person, a law-abiding citizen like me? Not who is the neighbor of some poor fellow who's attacked by robbers."

Jesus has a habit of taking conversations to places we don't want to go.

The expert in the law is forced to reply that his neighbor is "the one who showed him mercy" (v. 37).

My neighbor has suddenly become the one who shows

mercy.

This twist happens because this expert in the law wants to justify himself (v. 29). He's trying to gain eternal life through his works, and he wants to know if he's doing enough. He wants Jesus to tell him he's doing okay. Instead, through this story, Jesus tells him he needs to receive mercy from someone he despises—that is, Jesus.

Acknowledging we need help can be hard, but to receive it from someone we don't like is disconcerting.

Likewise, when Jesus has John write to the church at Laodicea, they probably also think Jesus knows them far too well. Laodicea is known for its banks, its wool and textile industry, plus its medical school, which develops ointments, including an eye salve.[4] Their letter is very specific.

> "You say, 'I am rich. I have everything I want. I don't need a thing!' And you don't realize that you are wretched and miserable and poor and blind and naked. So I advise you to buy gold from me—gold that has been purified by fire. Then you will be rich. Also buy white garments from me so you will not be shamed by your nakedness, and ointment for your eyes so you will be able to see."
> (Revelation 3:17–18)

Jesus addresses his message to their exact situation.

Even the words "since you are like lukewarm water, neither hot nor cold" (3:16) refer to Laodicea's water supply, which is piped from nearby towns and arrives lukewarm.[5] God puts his finger on the very things they believe give their town significance. Jesus makes such insightful comments, they leave us feeling exposed in his presence. Yet he exposes us not to shame us but to heal us, teach us, and encourage our faith.

Fully Known

Paul writes to the Corinthians, "All that I know now is partial and incomplete, but then I will know everything completely, just as God now knows me completely" (1 Corinthians 13:12).

For some it's a great delight to be fully known, for others it fills them with apprehension. When I first became a Christian, I was thrilled to realize God's all-knowing nature. He knew and understood me, often when I didn't understand myself or why I reacted the way I did. Human beings long for another who will truly know them, love them, and appreciate the uniqueness of their heart and mind. In Christ, I found that Someone. What a relief to know I was accepted with all my foibles and idiosyncrasies. And yet, there were times I found God getting a bit too close.

About six months after I became a Christian, I decided to buy myself a modern translation of the Bible, the same as my youth group friends. I saved up my pocket money and, one Saturday morning, caught the bus into town. I arrived at the Christian bookshop only to discover it was shut. The shop didn't open on Saturdays. It hadn't occurred to me to pray either before or after arriving at the closed shop. It hadn't crossed my mind that God would be interested.

With no other reason to be in town and the bus home some time off, I wandered into a supermarket. Perhaps I would buy a chocolate bar. I noticed on the wall opposite the cash registers a wire rack at about eye level. It contained contemporary paperback novels. To my astonishment, I noticed a lone Bible. The exact translation that I had planned to buy at the Christian bookshop. I picked it off the rack and confirmed it was the one I wanted. The price was as expected, so I bought it.

You might imagine I was excited about the way God had provided for me, but no, I left the supermarket thinking, "That was really weird."

On my way home, the analytical part of my brain kicked in, but I couldn't think of any explanation except that God had orchestrated this odd occurrence. But how?

Did he create a Bible out of nothing and put it on the shelf? This seemed unlikely.

Did God create a mistake in the order or delivery of the book? It's quite a bizarre mistake to confuse a thick Bible for a much thinner contemporary novel.

Yet the more puzzling question was why? Why did God care about an insignificant teenage girl who caught a bus into town to buy a Bible?

I didn't grow up in an emotionally close family, and I found the experience disconcerting, almost creepy. Why was God so interested in me? I didn't understand the personal nature of God.

I was happy for God to know about me, but not so comfortable with God knowing the personal details of my life. He knew I was going to town to buy a Bible. He knew the shop would be shut. He knew I would go to that supermarket, but I didn't know that. I felt God was getting a bit too involved in my life, a bit too close. It was unnerving.

These days I know God's intentions toward me are good and I can trust his interventions in my life. He loves me and wants to bless me with good things.

A. W. Tozer wrote, "He knows you individually as though there were not another person in the entire world. He died for you as certainly as if you had been the only lost one. He knows the worst about you and is the One who loves you the most."[6]

Jesus is indeed all-knowing. It's a wonderful blessing to be known and loved, yet it's also deeply challenging and causes some to create barriers that keep God at arm's length. Creating barriers occurs when we become more focused on gaining head knowledge about God instead of cultivating a relationship with him. It's the difference between reading a person's biography and knowing them personally. Jesus intends to destroy any barrier between us and God so we can come confidently into his presence.

> This High Priest of ours understands our weaknesses, for he faced all of the same testings we do, yet he did not sin. So let us come boldly to the throne of our gracious God. There we will receive his mercy, and we will find grace to help us when we need it most. (Hebrews 4:15–16)

However, some aren't ready to come to receive mercy and grace.

Jesus said to the Pharisees, "you search the Scriptures because you think they give you eternal life. But the Scriptures point to me! Yet you refuse to come to me to receive this life" (John 5:39–40). The Pharisees refuse to come to Jesus. He isn't the Messiah they expect or want. He doesn't fit their preconceived ideas. They don't come to him to have spiritual life.

Even now, sometimes I find coming into God's presence a little scary, though I know Jesus gives me access. I hear the daily news and know that other people's needs are much greater than mine. In comparison, my problems don't look important enough to bother Jesus. Unwittingly, I build barriers to keep God at a distance.

Creating barriers doesn't, of course, hinder God's knowledge of me, diminish his love for me, or stop him from pursuing me. However, it can disrupt my fellowship with him.

When we deny God access into the depths of our hearts, we lose confidence in his presence with us. The very thing Jesus desires most for us. He died "to bring you to God" (1 Peter 3:18 NIV).

Jesus in Pain

Ultimately, Jesus's identification with us leads him to the garden of Gethsemane, where he voluntarily obeys his Father's will, even when it clashes with his own desires. Before the soldiers arrive to arrest him, Jesus prays, "Father, if you are willing, please take this cup of suffering away from me. Yet I want your will to be done, not mine" (Luke 22:42). In response, an angel appears from heaven to strengthen him (v. 43).

When a whole detachment of soldiers arrives to arrest him, Peter draws a sword. Jesus says, "Put your sword back into its sheath. Shall I not drink from the cup of suffering the Father has given me?" (John 18:11).

Jesus doesn't lay down his life lightly. Nor is the situation out of his control. He's fully aware of what will happen and prewarns his disciples (Matthew 20:18).

We can approach God's throne boldly because we know Jesus became one of us to die and break the power of the devil. He understands, so we know he will always support us, strengthen us, sustain us. "For only as a human being could he die, and only by dying could he break the power of the devil, who had the power of death" (Hebrews 2:14).

Jesus became human. He continues to identify with us. He knows our world. He knows us.

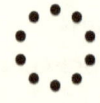

Let's Pray

Thank you, Lord, that you cared enough to leave heaven and become one of us. Thank you for this extraordinary act of identification and for experiencing an ordinary life for thirty years before you embarked on your true mission.

May your experience of family encourage me when I feel unsupported and alone.

When your messages get a bit too personal, remind me that you don't want to shame me but to heal me and teach me. You do fully know me. Help me to always see this as a blessing so I don't try to hide from you.

Reveal any lies that prevent me from coming into your presence with the assurance of your acceptance. Help me to walk in your truth and protect me from the devil's subtle deceptions.

In Jesus's name.

Amen.

5.

God Loves

God loves you.

Maybe you already know that. Perhaps you've been told for a very long time that God loves you. But does knowing that God loves you make any difference in your life? Or is it only a truth you hold in your mind? Does it make a difference when you wake up on Monday morning, when you watch the evening news, or when you're facing difficulties?

Often at wedding services, we listen to Paul's description of love in 1 Corinthians 13:4–7, but it can also apply to God's love. God "is patient and kind." God "is not jealous or boastful or proud or rude." God "does not demand [his] own way." God "is not irritable," and he "keeps no record of being wronged." God "does not rejoice about injustice but rejoices whenever the truth wins out." God "never gives up, never loses faith, is always hopeful, and endures through every circumstance."

I wonder if this is how you see God?

Let's do a little test to see if you really know God loves you.

John tells us, "Such love has no fear, because perfect love expels all fear. If we are afraid, it is for fear of punishment, and this shows that we have not fully experienced his perfect love" (1 John 4:18).

Here's the test: Are you afraid of anything?

John tells us if we're completely convinced of God's love, we won't be afraid. God intends for us to live a life free of fear because we know we're loved.

I don't know about you, but I'm not there yet. The other day I was hanging the clothes out to dry. Our clothesline is attached to the rear wall of our house, so I had my back to the garden. Behind me was a strip of lawn, and beyond that was a garden bed with automatic sprinklers. All of a sudden, I heard a hissing sound. I nearly jumped out of my skin. I looked behind me expecting to see a snake. Instead, all I saw were the sprinklers spraying water.

When my logical mind kicked in, I realized that the hissing sound was far too loud to be a snake. I felt like God had sent me a little object lesson to let me know that I still have many fears. Nevertheless, I'm not as fearful as I used to be.

At the first church where Ross served as a pastor, I was asked to speak one day to a small group of women. I spent weeks preparing, but when I got up to speak, my mind seemed to stop working. I left out half my talk and sat down. I told God I would never speak in public again.

Never say never to God! Since that time, I have spoken dozens of times in different settings. Knowing God loves me helped me overcome my fears.

God loves us—completely, unconditionally, extravagantly, endlessly.

This truth overwhelms me when I reflect on it. Every true love ever recorded in song, story, or poem contains a smidgen of truth about the way God feels about me.

Free from Fear

We don't generally associate our fears with not knowing God's love. However, our fears expose our underlying beliefs. Our fears tell us we aren't convinced God takes care of us, acts in our best interests, and knows what's best for us. Fear also tells us God's protection might be based on our performance. Our performance might not be good enough, and God might penalize us for our failings.

The truth is God's love is based on his character, not on our performance, faithfulness, or love for him. Blaise Pascal, a seventeenth-century theologian, is credited with saying, "If you knew, really knew, how much God loved you, not one fear would remain in your heart."[1]

There are times when I hesitate to embrace God's love because I know that while God loves me as I am, he won't leave me as he finds me. He wants "to present [the church] to himself as a glorious church without a spot or wrinkle or any other blemish. Instead, she will be holy and without fault" (Ephesians 5:27).

God is working to make us a glorious church, so he shines his light into the dark corners of our lives and reveals the things he wants to remove or cleanse. This isn't a pleasant process. We might respond by shying away from his love.

Jesus describes God as the Gardener who prunes us (John 15:1–2). Biblical authors describe him as the blazing fire that refines us (Malachi 3:2) and the Father who disciplines us (Hebrews 12:9–11).

God uses images for the growth process that are

painful. The process of being pruned, refined, and disciplined shows up as various kinds of difficulties. When I experience problems, my first thought is where's God? Has he abandoned me? Does he really love me?

I responded this way when my husband, Ross, was diagnosed with cancer and also when I've experienced lesser difficulties, such as problems at the churches we have pastored. Fortunately, these days I stop and consider my history with God. I remind myself of God's character and his ways. When I find I'm being pruned, refined, and disciplined, I tell myself God loves me and will never allow anything to cross my path that won't ultimately benefit me.

God the Good Parent

God treats us like good parents treat their children. However, loving parents make unpleasant, even painful, decisions their children don't understand. Parents might move to another town to ensure their children have a better future, but all the children understand is their loss of friends.

Once, the bank where Ross worked informed us we had to move because of a restructuring of their resources. One of my children became particularly upset, and I suggested we pray about it.

"What would you like me to pray?" I asked.

"I want to live near the school so I can walk there."

I immediately saw a problem. We expected to move to a small town and were therefore unlikely to have a choice as to where we lived. Ross would be the bank manager and required to live in the manager's residence. Most country towns have their schools close to the shopping area, but the banks were moving their managers' residences away from the town center for security reasons. Having offered to pray, I could hardly back down, so I prayed for a house near a school.

We moved to Corryong. The bank was across the road from the school, and the manager's residence was next door to the bank, the old arrangement. We couldn't have been any closer to the school. God answered my child's prayer. Years later, I chatted about this move with my child. They had completely forgotten their prayer! God answered the prayer more for my benefit than theirs.

Loving parents might make their children take medicine, receive injections, and visit the dentist, even if it causes them temporary pain. If a child is seriously unwell, parents might take them to the hospital for surgery, chemotherapy, or other painful procedures. They act in the best interests of their child. When children grow up in a loving and supportive environment, they learn to trust their parents even when they don't understand the decisions they make. Likewise, God sometimes allows the pain of living in a broken world into our lives, but it doesn't mean he doesn't love us or care about us. He acts in our best interest.

God is a good parent who protects us from unnecessary harm, but not always from pain.

When you feel afraid or you start to doubt God's love, imagine yourself as a little child completely loved by your parents. Imagine how safe and secure you would feel. That's how God wants us to feel—safe and secure in his love. He wants us to open our hearts and receive his great love so we can be free from fear.

Intimacy

God greatly desires for us to know the depth and breadth of his love, so he uses intimate images to describe our relationship with him. Jeremiah describes God's people first as a bride (Jeremiah 2:2) but then as a prostitute (v. 20). He berates God's people because they abandon God and worship foreign gods (v. 25). Jeremiah illustrates their faithlessness by using the term "adultery" (3:6). Poor Hosea becomes a living object lesson to the Israelites when God tells him to marry an adulterous wife (Hosea 1:2 NIV).

> **God freely employs the intimate symbols of marriage and sex to demonstrate how he feels about his people.**

These days, people tend to crave wealth, prestige, or beauty rather than wooden idols, but whenever we desire something more than God, we run the risk of being spiritual adulterers. This powerful imagery doesn't stop with the prophets.

Paul explains to the Corinthians, "I am jealous for you with a godly jealousy. I promised you to one husband, to Christ, so that I might present you as a pure virgin to him" (2 Corinthians 11:2 NIV). God desires the closest possible relationship with his people.

In love, God woos, calls, cleanses, restores, heals, molds,

prunes, purifies, and disciplines us. When his love meets our brokenness, we may feel pain. Allowing God's love to invade the deep recesses of our hearts may feel scary. Yet if we let his love dissolve our fear, we open the way for our pain to be relieved and for healing and wholeness to come into our hearts and lives.

Without the Right Motivation

God so desires relationship with us, he doesn't even wait for us to get our motivation right. We see the father's quick response to the prodigal son, even when the son's motivation for going home was hunger, not repentance (Luke 15:17). The woman at the well came for water, not compassion (John 4:7). The woman caught in adultery didn't even come to Jesus voluntarily (John 8:3). However, Jesus accepts them and shows them love before they even think about repenting.

God is pleased when our heart responds to him. He so desires to shower us with his love that he doesn't even wait for us to repent before he accepts us. In fact, true repentance happens only when we admit the extent to which our sins have hurt the ones we love and realize we never want to hurt them again.

Peter preaches a stinging Pentecost sermon. Yet only when people's hearts are "pierced" does Peter say, "repent" (Acts 2:37–38). Until we encounter the love of God in the depths of our hearts, we cannot consistently leave our wrongdoing behind.

We're changed not by the threat of punishment but by an overwhelming sense of gratitude.

Obstacles that Steal

Obstacles may steal our ability to trust God's love. We might question God's love when we read the Old Testament, which seems to present God differently from the compassionate Jesus we see in the Gospels.

Shortly after I became a Christian, a rather intimidating preacher encouraged us to read the whole Bible in our first year as a believer. I'm an avid reader, so I did. However, my lack of knowledge of Jewish history meant I incorrectly assumed that God's people constantly ended up in exile. As I read each of the prophetic books, God warned them about their idolatry or their oppression of the poor or both, and clearly the people didn't respond. Every time I read how they failed to respond, I pictured them marching across the desert into captivity. Then I read the promises of return and saw them walking back across the desert. Back and forth, back and forth, I imagined them trudging across the desert.

Years later, I learned the tribes making up Israel and Judah each experienced exile only once. I was surprised. I had seriously underestimated the extent of God's patience, compassion, and mercy.

God is just like Jesus. This is his self-description:

> Yahweh! The Lord! The God of compassion and mercy! I am slow to anger and filled with unfailing love and faithfulness. I lavish unfailing love to a thousand generations.

I forgive iniquity, rebellion, and sin. (Exodus 34:6–7)

God is "compassionate and gracious," "slow to anger, abounding in love" (v. 6 NIV). Our minds seem to gravitate toward occasions in the Old Testament when God enacts his judgment. The law and punishments God imparts to Moses seem harsh because we underestimate God's holiness. We fail to understand his actions because we overlook his deep offense at people's sin.

God is holy and just. Every sin is worthy of the death penalty.

Any time someone doesn't die because of their sin, they're being shown mercy (Ezekiel 18:4). Often, the punishments given under Moses aren't carried out to their full extent because God keeps on showing mercy. For example, David and Bathsheba should've been stoned for adultery. God looked forward to the day when Jesus would take upon himself the entire penalty for sin.

When someone experiences God's punishment—like the sudden deaths of Uzzah, who touches the ark of the covenant (2 Samuel 6:6–7), Nadab and Abihu, who offer unauthorized fire (Leviticus 10:1–2), and Ananias and Sapphira, who lie to the Holy Spirit (Acts 5:1–11)—we feel stunned because we take God's mercy for granted. These incidents serve as severe reminders of God's holiness.

Examples of God's mercy abound throughout the Old

Testament—Cain's protection from retaliation (Genesis 4:15), Ruth's acceptance even though she's a Moabite (Deuteronomy 23:3), Rahab's inclusion despite being a Canaanite (Deuteronomy 7:2) and a prostitute (Joshua 2:1), and God's forgiveness of Nineveh, ignoring Jonah's displeasure (Jonah 4:2). Through it all God doesn't change. He's still "the God of compassion and mercy."

In the book of Revelation, we see a day is coming when God will again enact his judgment. There will be justice, but we can trust God's character. He will act justly but also with compassion and mercy.

For a Little While

Another obstacle to trusting God's love is that we live with a partial separation. In the book of Philemon, we find the story of Onesimus, Philemon's slave. He steals from Philemon and runs away to Rome. In the providence of God, he meets Paul and subsequently becomes a Christian. Paul sends Onesimus back to Philemon and writes, "It seems you lost Onesimus for a little while so that you could have him back forever. He is no longer like a slave to you. He is more than a slave, for he is a beloved brother" (Philemon 1:15–16).

Due to Onesimus's sin, he and Philemon become separated "for a little while." This illustrates in a small way our separation from God. We receive a glimpse into the age-old theological question: Why did God allow sin to enter his perfect world, which then separated people from God?

In God's economy of time, the separation is only "for a little while." God has a plan to restore the relationship, and not just to restore it but to make it more intimate—no longer slaves but friends (John 15:15).

For us to fully grasp the depths of God's compassion and mercy, God allows evil to enter his perfect world so we could see how he would deal with such a crisis. There's no other way we could learn about the extent of God's amazing love except through the extreme measure of allowing the devastation of sin and evil.

In the garden of Eden, Adam and Eve know God's holiness and justice. But "perfect" justice means that Adam and Eve live under a death threat. One bad choice, no second chances, and one sin causes the process of death to begin. While Adam and Eve live in a state of perfection, their relationship with God is somewhat slavelike. God couldn't confide in them the way he would like to because they couldn't know the depths of his compassion and mercy.

We learn more about someone when we go through tough times together than when all is going well. Going through tough times at churches with Ross brought us closer together. We refined our priorities and found ourselves in agreement on important matters. We had the same desire for the church to grow, and we understood what it would take, even when others didn't.

Without Adam and Eve's disobedience, we couldn't understand the damage of sin and the cost to God of reconciliation. Consequently, we couldn't appreciate the extent of God's love.

Through the cross, we learn how valuable we are to him and how much he loves us.

God desires close relationships with his people, and he will go to extraordinary lengths to achieve this purpose. Now that justice has been put in place through Jesus's death, God can respond the way he has always wanted, with compassion. The garden of Eden was a graceless place, nevertheless, we see God acting in grace by making clothes for Adam and Eve (Genesis 3:21).

When God describes our future home, he does so in terms of a city, "the holy city, Jerusalem, descending out of heaven from God" (Revelation 21:10). God won't take us back to the garden but rather to a "city with eternal foundations, a city designed and built by God" (Hebrews 11:10). A city with foundations speaks of permanence, security, and community. We're gaining more than we lost. "The story of mankind starts in a garden but ends in a celestial city. He is not just saved but is promised a state of glory."[2]

Loving God for Himself

We understand God's love more completely when we compare it to human love. The tragic story of Saul's daughter, Michal, begins when she falls in love with David (1 Samuel 18:20). Michal's father, King Saul, tells David he can become his son-in-law if he kills a hundred Philistines. Saul, who is secretly jealous of David, hopes he dies in the conflict. When he doesn't, Saul has no choice but to give Michal to David as his wife.

When Saul's jealousy turns to murderous intent toward David, Michal helps David escape from her father (19:11). Then, in David's absence, Saul gives her in marriage to Palti since Saul never wanted David as a son-in-law (25:44).

About fifteen years later, after Saul's death, David demands that Michal be given back to him. "So Ishbosheth [Saul's son] took Michal away from her husband, Palti son of Laish. Palti followed along behind her as far as Bahurim, weeping as he went" (2 Samuel 3:15–16).

David's actions seem to be a political move to form an alliance with Saul's house. After all, David already has six other wives (vv. 2–5).

The second time around, we never see Michal happy about being David's wife, and she speaks to him with disdain (6:20). The evidence suggests she prefers being the wife of an ordinary person like Palti, who loves her with a great passion, than to have the privilege of being one of King David's many wives. David, it seems, wants Michal only for her connections, whereas Palti wants her because of love.

Consider the challenge, do we love God for himself? Or do we love him only for his benefits?

Love in Action

How can we know if God really loves us?

How do we know if another person loves us? Mostly because they tell us and want to spend time with us. However, the real test is in their actions. If love doesn't show up in a person's actions toward another, they don't love them, regardless of their words. In the area of domestic violence, we see this tragically played out. Women often stay in abusive situations because their abusers tell them they love them and want to be with them. This isn't love. It's control. You don't persistently hurt someone you love.

Additionally, love doesn't force the receiver to accept the love being offered.

We know that God loves us because he gives us the freedom to choose not to love him in return. The decision to accept or refuse God's love is ours alone.

Furthermore, we make sacrifices for those we love.

I enjoyed the TV detective series *Castle*, which aired some years ago. I like mysteries, and I enjoyed the context because the main character, Rick Castle, was an author. Even more than that, I found it romantic. Castle was prepared to sacrifice so much of his time and money to help Detective Beckett solve murders because he loved her. And it changed him. Gradually over a couple of series, he gave up his flamboyant playboy ways and became more responsible. That's what happens when we love someone. We change and become less selfish.

God also shows his love through sacrificial actions. "He gave his one and only Son" (John 3:16).

God gave up the most precious thing of all, his Son—an enormous expense, an enormous action, an enormous sacrifice—so we can know beyond any doubt that God loves us. A God who would freely give up his own Son must have good intentions.

Paul gave this instruction to husbands: "Love your wives, just as Christ loved the church. He gave up his life for her" (Ephesians 5:25). Again, love is described in terms of sacrifice. If someone is prepared to give up something precious for our sake, then we know they do love us.

Sometimes we think we need more power to live the Christian life, but Paul prayed the Ephesians would have power to understand the vastness of Christ's love (3:17–19). Knowing God loves us is the only way we will ever trust him and live as he intends. Entrusting our lives to someone without being convinced of their love and good motives is incredibly difficult. However, when we firmly believe someone loves us and has good intentions, we will trust that person, even if they allow painful things to come into our lives.

Let's Pray

Thank you, Lord, for your unfailing love. I pray the truth of your love won't stay just in my head but will move into my heart and to the depths of my soul. Help me accept your love and allow it to flow into the deep recesses of my heart to heal me, restore me, and purify me.

Thank you, Lord, that you are a good Father who has only good intentions toward me. Remind me that your sacrifice on the cross shows me how much I am loved.

When the Bible seems harsh, help me to understand what you're saying to your people then and now.

Thank you, Lord, that all my fears can be driven away when I receive your perfect love.

In Jesus's name.

Amen.

6

God Gives Hope

As a child, I always celebrated with my parents on New Year's Eve. They would go to a friend's place or an organized event. I loved it! I enjoyed staying up until midnight. I liked standing around singing *Auld Lang Syne*. Even though I didn't know what it meant, the song conveyed a sense of companionship. I loved the way people connected and wished each other a happy new year. I also liked the idea of a fresh start—new calendars, blank planners, and empty diaries that held the promise of good things to come.

Somewhere in adolescence, I became disillusioned. I realized that even in January, people are diagnosed with cancer, marriages fail, and disasters happen. All the positive good wishes are empty promises, wishful thinking, a crossing of fingers.

"I hope you have a good year."
"I hope you have good health."
"I hope you have good luck."

Yet, the word *hope* in this context, has no substance, no reason to expect anything good. Being without hope leads to fear and anxiety.

In contrast, biblical hope is an "anchor for our souls" (Hebrews 6:19). It looks back to the cross, where God interrupted history to restore our relationship with him, and looks forward to the time when God will again enter history to bring justice and restoration. Hope is an anchor because it holds us to God—"the eternal Rock" (Isaiah 26:4).

When I visited Israel in 2014, our Jewish tour guide told us the word *rock* in Israel always means bedrock. All other rocks are called stones, no matter how big they are, because they're potentially moveable. God is our Bedrock, our security, our safe place.

God gives hope—a hope that is sure, steadfast, and unshakable despite upheavals in our lives.

Hope—Not Just for Now

When I first experienced God's love and forgiveness as a teenager, I found real hope. A lightness came into my life where previously I'd felt emptiness and futility. Now I believed in a God who cared about me, forgave me, and showed interest in me. I didn't understand why Paul would say "if our hope in Christ is only for this life, we are more to be pitied than anyone in the world" (1 Corinthians 15:19).

My emotional state changed so beneficially by becoming a Christian that I didn't care if it lasted for only this life. Later, as I matured, I began reading newspapers and listening to the media. I became aware that hardships and tragedies made sense only from the perspective of heaven.

Paul describes himself as pressed, perplexed, hunted, and knocked down (2 Corinthians 4:8–9). Yet he takes the divine perspective. "For our light and momentary troubles are achieving for us an eternal glory that far outweighs them all" (v. 17 NIV).

Later Paul itemizes his specific troubles. He receives thirty-nine lashes on five occasions, is beaten with rods three times, is stoned and shipwrecked, and spends twenty-four hours adrift at sea. He lives with dangers from rivers, robbers, relatives, gentiles, and false brothers. He goes without sleep, food, and water. He often experiences insufficient shelter. In addition, he felt concern for the churches (11:24–28).

And yet Paul considers these troubles "light and momentary"!

Paul looks at his troubles from the perspective of eternity and thinks about the long-term purposes of God. He focuses on the big picture. If Paul's hope isn't in Christ and the knowledge that one day he would be with him, he wouldn't cope with these difficulties.

The world hopes tomorrow will bring better circumstances, but Christians hope in Christ and Christ alone. "He alone is my rock and my salvation, my fortress where I will never be shaken ... my hope is in him" (Psalm 62:2, 5).

Tomorrow may not bring better circumstances. Tomorrow didn't bring better circumstances for Paul. Historians believe he died for his faith, and Paul sees this coming (2 Timothy 4:6). If our hope is in Christ, we can learn to live confidently today and face whatever the future may bring.

Recently, I rewatched the movie *Cast Away*. At the start of the movie, the main character, Chuck Noland, is a workaholic obsessed with time. After being shipwrecked and living for four years on a deserted island, he returns to civilization a different person with a more realistic perspective.[1] As I watched the movie, a thought occurred to me. Isn't this what God does to us? He allows difficult circumstances to grow us. And if that means sitting on an isolated island for four years, so be it.

Future glory outweighs present inconveniences.

I struggle to understand a God who operates with such long time frames.

Yet God's long-term perspective means he acts in my best interests in the present. God calls us to enlarge our picture of him and his purposes so he can give us real hope. When our hope comes from God, we can trust that he will use our present problems to bring us future blessings.

Future Glory

Our ultimate hope is in God's promise of justice and restoration. In the book of Revelation, John receives a prophetic vision of future events that gradually unfolds. John writes, "I began to weep bitterly because no one was found worthy to open the scroll and read it" (Revelation 5:4). Opening the scroll would usher in the future. Jesus is revealed as the only one worthy to open it, but when he does, it unleashes such waves of destruction that we may wonder why it needs to be opened at all. Breaking the seals on the scroll initiates the events that lead to the culmination of world history. John weeps because if the scroll isn't opened, we would remain stuck in a broken world with no hope for the future.

Jesus explains with this illustration: "It will be like a woman suffering the pains of labor. When her child is born, her anguish gives way to joy because she has brought a new baby into the world" (John 16:21).

One day, we will experience such joy in the eternal "city designed and built by God" (Hebrews 11:10) we will forget any anguish we experienced here on earth. Of course, this doesn't mean we don't try to alleviate suffering and help those in need. But it does mean we're never overwhelmed since "this world as we know it will soon pass away" (1 Corinthians 7:31).

We can make sense of destruction and devastation only if we take the long-term view. The book of Revelation makes it clear that God is on the throne controlling world events. We can trust him even when sad things happen because a new day is coming when God will wipe every tear from our eyes (Revelation 21:4).

Obstacles to Hope

While we wait for this new day, we cultivate biblical hope. Property, cars, bank investments, jewelry, achievements, and relationships can give us a taste of security and attempt to steal our hope in God. However, God doesn't want his people relying on worldly or temporal things for security since this causes anxiety, not hope.

Even when God gives instructions about the land he allots to the Israelites, he tells them that their earthly inheritance isn't permanent. "The land must never be sold on a permanent basis, for the land belongs to me. You are only foreigners and tenant farmers working for me" (Leviticus 25:23). Even today in Israel most of the land is owned by the government.

What happens if those who hope to find satisfaction in their jobs are made redundant? Or those who find confidence in their appearance grow old? Or those whose worth is connected to a spouse who dies before them?

Cultivating hope is difficult when we rely on our own resources.

When Ross, my husband, was diagnosed with cancer, my level of anxiety skyrocketed because my security was in him and his ability to provide for me. Over the coming months and years, I learned how to put my hope in God. As Christians, we may feel shaken when unexpected tragedies happen, but when our hope is in God, we aren't in despair because he is our security. Whatever happens, he will be with us, supporting us, and caring for us.

> I will never fail you.
> I will never abandon you.
> (Hebrews 13:5)

Developing this kind of hope can also be difficult if we trust in our achievements. If we were to become paralyzed and never able to do another thing for God's kingdom, he would still love us. God values us for who we are, not what we do. "For you are a chosen people. You are royal priests, a holy nation, God's very own possession" (1 Peter 2:9). "See what great love the Father has lavished on us, that we should be called children of God!" (1 John 3:1 NIV).

Looking for worldly things to satisfy our deeper needs for self-respect, fulfillment, or significance is a modern form of idol worship. God provides for our needs to be met in our relationship with him, and herein is our hope. God is our "sure foundation" (Isaiah 33:6).

"In peace I will lie down and sleep, for you alone, O Lord, will keep me safe" (Psalm 4:8). God is our constant—our robust rock, our firm fortress, our hardy hope.

Hope Beyond Our Senses

If we believe only what we see and hear with our physical senses, our hope will be fragile. Our eyes and ears don't always give us an accurate picture or all the information we need.

I have a magician friend who does tricks with balls and coins. Sometimes when I watch him, coins seem to appear from nowhere and balls vanish. I realize afresh my eyes don't always tell me the whole truth or give me the complete picture. The magician's skill and quickness deceive my eyes. Likewise, the reality of the spiritual life is more than what I see.

> For we are not fighting against flesh-and-blood enemies, but against evil rulers and authorities of the unseen world, against mighty powers in this dark world, and against evil spirits in the heavenly places. (Ephesians 6:12)

We don't see spiritual realities with human eyes. Only God has the true vantage point.

Research has shown that motion sickness is caused by our brains receiving conflicting information from our eyes and ears since our ears control our sense of balance. When I suffer from motion sickness, apparently I need to focus on the movement or shut my eyes (provided I'm not the one who's driving!). Shutting my eyes removes the conflict, and I rely only on my sense of balance. I've found this remedy quite successful, though highly inconvenient if I'm on a scenic trip.

Likewise, we "shut our eyes" to the way we see ourselves, even if it feels uncomfortable, and believe God's true picture of ourselves and our world. God sees us as his chosen people, holy and loved (Colossians 3:12). God sees our world as temporary and passing away (2 Corinthians 4:18). This is the true picture, and it gives great hope. All else is a false impression that can give us spiritual motion sickness.

Hope in Hopelessness

We can even find hope in situations that appear hopeless. Jesus chooses an unlikely group of disciples to be agents of hope in the world. Rather than choose disciples from one of the religious groups, such as the Pharisees, who were known to study the Scriptures (John 5:39), Jesus chose ordinary men, such as fishermen and a tax collector.

After the Day of Pentecost, when Peter and John preach and teach in the Temple, the council of the rulers and elders, and teachers of religious law meet to discuss the situation. They are astonished that they are "ordinary men with no special training in the Scriptures" (Acts 4:13).

What hope does this motley group of disciples have of establishing God's kingdom on earth?

Let's take a closer look at these people who transform the world. "These are the twelve he chose: Simon (whom he named Peter), James and John (the sons of Zebedee, but Jesus nicknamed them "Sons of Thunder"), Andrew, Philip, Bartholomew, Matthew, Thomas, James (son of Alphaeus), Thaddaeus, Simon (the zealot), Judas Iscariot (who later betrayed him)" (Mark 3:16–19).

Two disciples have the name James, one the brother of John and son of Zebedee and one the son of Alphaeus. (A third James, the brother of Jesus, is mentioned later.)

The only thing we know about this second James is his father's name, Alphaeus. Matthew, the tax collector (also known as Levi), is likewise called the son of Alphaeus (Mark 2:14). James and Matthew may be brothers or stepbrothers. James may also be a Zealot along with Thaddaeus, Simon (the zealot), and Judas Iscariot.[2]

The Zealots are a political group who believe the best way to free Israel from Roman oppression is through armed revolt. Zealots hate the presence of Romans in their land and hate those who cooperate with them, like ... tax collectors. Jesus had not only Zealots and tax collectors as disciples but also a couple of fishermen in need of anger management (Luke 9:54) and one who speaks even when he doesn't know what to say (Mark 9:5–6).

Yet Jesus's followers change the world.

The group Jesus chooses has every reason to disintegrate into factions. Yet, he manages to galvanize them by focusing on the one thing they have in common—hope in God's promised kingdom. Their hope means they're prepared to put aside their prejudices and agendas for God's kingdom to come (except for Judas).

These days, the church is called to do the same thing. Put aside our prejudices and agendas to focus on the beliefs we share and commit to God's kingdom. Some days I wonder if God isn't hindering the process, as he often chooses leaders who don't naturally work well together. Fortunately, our hope isn't in people's leadership ability but in God's ability to bring about his purposes.

Stolen Hope

For some, like Abram's second wife, Hagar, the little hope she has is taken from her. Hagar is a gentile, a woman, and a slave (Genesis 16:1–2). (Later Pharisees would commonly thank God they aren't any of these.[3]) Hagar's life seems doomed by a lack of opportunities. Yet surely her status will improve when she becomes pregnant with Abram's child. But she is mistreated by Sarai and flees (v. 6). Nevertheless God finds her and allows her to name him El Roi—the God who sees me. She is told to name her son Ishmael, which means "God hears" (vv. 11–14). We have a God who sees and hears even the cries of a female, gentile slave.

If our hope is stolen by others or by circumstances, we can still find comfort and hope in an all-seeing and all-hearing God. Many in our world are mistreated by those who commit crimes known only to God, including domestic violence and sexual abuse. However, we can rest in the assurance that we have an all-knowing God who cares. "Break the arm of the wicked man; call the evildoer to account for his wickedness that would not otherwise be found out" (Psalm 10:15 NIV). Nothing is hidden from God. While the wicked person may be able to fool some, God knows what goes on in secret.

This psalm gives us a vivid description of the evildoer and reminds us that God will bring justice (v. 18). He helps victims who put their trust in him and his ways (v. 14). "The Lord is close to the brokenhearted; he rescues those whose spirits are crushed" (Psalm 34:18).

God sees our distress and hears our cries.

Never Too Late

When we look at Jonah in his helpless state inside a great fish, we may think it's too late for hope. Yet Jonah prays, "As my life was slipping away, I remembered the Lord. And my earnest prayer went out to you in your holy Temple" (Jonah 2:7).

His words remind me of the opening lines of the poem "The Great Mercy" by Katharine Tynan.

> Betwixt the saddle and the ground
> Was mercy sought and mercy found.
> Yea, in the twinkling of an eye,
> He cried; and Thou hast heard his cry.[4]

It takes only a "twinkling of an eye" to cry out to the Lord—only the briefest fraction of a second to acknowledge God. When the thief on the cross said, "Jesus, remember me when you come into your Kingdom" (Luke 23:42), he receives Jesus's assurance of eternal life. God's eagerness to cover us with mercy is so relentless it may not happen until the last instant of a person's life. We'll never know this side of eternity who cries out to God in their dying moments.

Jonah's cry leads to the return of his physical life, and he shows his gratitude with "songs of praise" (Jonah 2:9) even before he finds himself on dry land. A restored relationship with God is more precious than the continuance of physical life.

Some wait to the point of death to cry out to God, which is regrettable. Yet even then, God is willing to bestow mercy.

It's never too late to hope in God.

Rewarded

According to Hebrews 11:6, "Anyone who wants to come to him must believe that God exists and ..." And what?

Instinctively what would you expect to come next? Anyone who comes to God must believe he exists and ... must obey him? ... must love him?

No, the rest of the verse says, "... and that he rewards those who sincerely seek him." God wants us to believe he will reward us for seeking him. Our hope is also based on God's promise of rewards. Faith isn't entirely altruistic.

Is this the only reason to seek God? While we can expect God to reward us, that isn't why we worship him. To illustrate this balance, it's helpful to remember that God is our Father. At Christmas, many of us spend time with our parents or children because of who they are, but we might also expect them to bless us with a gift. We would visit them regardless of whether they gave us a gift or not, but it's a joy to receive from them. Likewise, with God, we commit our lives to him because of who he is, but we also enjoy the gifts he gives us, and we can expect more blessings.

God rewards his people.

Jesus tells a parable in which he rewards his faithful servants with leadership (Luke 19:17). And throughout the New Testament we find phrases like "great reward" (Luke 6:23), and "receive your full reward" (2 John v. 8). The idea of accolades seems to be a much stronger thought in the minds of the New Testament writers than in ours.

These writers encourage us to be like Moses, who was looking forward to his reward.

> Moses, when he grew up, refused to be called the son of Pharaoh's daughter. He chose to share the oppression of God's people instead of enjoying the fleeting pleasures of sin. He thought it was better to suffer for the sake of Christ than to own the treasures of Egypt, for he was looking ahead to his great reward. (Hebrews 11:24–26)

God hasn't called us to a completely selfless life, rather he expects us to anticipate blessings, even in this life. The rewards we experience may not be what the world values. Instead, they may be deeper friendships, satisfying work, enjoyable leisure, and the sense of God's presence in our lives. We can work enthusiastically for the Lord, for we know that nothing we do for him is ever useless (1 Corinthians 15:58).

Andrew Klavan's memoir, *The Great Good Thing*, is the story of how a secular Jew became a Christian. Klavan's was a long, slow journey to faith. After many years, he got to the point of believing intellectually there must be a God, so one night he decided to pray. He was in a good place in his life. He had a good job, a loving family, and a nice place to live, so he simply prayed "Thank you, God" and fell asleep.

The next morning, he knew something had changed. He felt a sense of joy he hadn't experienced before. He took one small step toward God, prayed a sincere prayer, and God rewarded his faith.[5]

Certain Hope

God gives us many reminders to have hope, like my roses. They're resilient, flower often, and need only periodic pruning. This is good because I'm not much of a gardener.

The first winter I pruned them, I wondered whether they would ever bloom again. They looked so dead. But sure enough, the weather changed and so did they. I prune with greater confidence now because I have a certain hope.

Biblical hope is a certain hope, an anchor for our souls. Peter encouraged his readers with this hope.

> Praise be to the God and Father of our Lord

Jesus Christ! In his great mercy he has given us new birth into a living hope through the resurrection of Jesus Christ from the dead, and into an inheritance that can never perish, spoil or fade. (1 Peter 1:3-4 NIV)

We have a living hope. A hope that looks back to the resurrection of Jesus and forward to our inheritance.

Let's Pray

Thank you, Lord, that my hope in you is an anchor for my soul.

Thank you, Lord, for the cross, which gives me hope that I am valued by you and that you have good things in mind for me. Thank you, too, that I can look forward with hope to the time when you will again enter history to bring justice and restoration.

Thank you, Lord, for the promise of reward. May I keep this in mind when following your ways becomes difficult.

I pray that the hope that I have in you, will make a difference in the way I live. Help me be a person of optimism and peace, not anxiety or fear, despite what is going on in the world.

In Jesus's name.
Amen.

7

God Has a Plan

My husband, Ross, began pastoral ministry in 1993. Ten years earlier, he applied to a theological seminary on two separate occasions, but he wasn't accepted. This devastated us at the time because we had a strong conviction that this was God's plan for us.

Friends told us, "Don't worry. God has a plan. If he shuts one door, he will open another." These words were well intentioned but not helpful, especially when nothing happened for a very long time. As time passed and Ross still wasn't in ministry, I began to wonder about God's plans.

Are God's plans scheduled or spontaneous?

Are they fixed or flexible?

Are they specific or sketchy?

Bill Watterson, the creator of *Calvin and Hobbes*, said, "God put me on earth to accomplish certain things. Right now, I'm so far behind, I'll never die."[1]

Are God's plans a to-do list?

Our lives may seem like a mishmash of events that bear no resemblance to any sort of plan. We may begin to think we must've somehow missed God's plan for our lives. Or perhaps we're paralyzed by indecision because we fear making a choice that might take us away from God's plan. God indeed has a plan, but it's far greater and more remarkable than we realize.

God has a plan. It's a vast, amazing, all-encompassing, eternal plan.

Some people find this a great comfort. We aren't wandering around aimlessly through life—there's meaning and purpose. Others find it a great challenge. What if God's plan for me includes being a missionary or a monk? God's plans are both a comfort and a challenge.

Yet God invites us to engage in this plan. It's a call to adventure, and we never quite know how it's going to turn out. Are we up for the challenge?

Special Treasure

God's overarching plan starts before time begins (Ephesians 1:4), and it unfolds throughout the books of the Bible. In the Old Testament, God chooses the Israelites to be his people. "You will be my own special treasure from among all the peoples on earth; for all the earth belongs to me. And you will be my kingdom of priests, my holy nation" (Exodus 19:5–6).

God plans for the Israelites to show the world how good it is to live God's way.

Even so, it isn't enough to be chosen. The Israelites also have to choose God and exercise faith to be in relationship with him (Romans 10:16–18). And while the Israelites are God's chosen people, he intends to bless all nations through them (Genesis 12:3).

Paul explains, "The Scriptures looked forward to this

time when God would make the Gentiles right in his sight because of their faith. God proclaimed this good news to Abraham long ago when he said, 'All nations will be blessed through you'" (Galatians 3:8).

God includes Ruth and Rahab, who aren't Israelites but become part of God's people (Ruth; Joshua 2, 6). He sends Jonah to pagan Nineveh (Jonah 1), and other prophets bring God's messages to Egypt (Ezekiel 29) and Edom (Obadiah). God desires for all nations to repent and choose to follow his ways. He looks forward to heaven filled with "a vast crowd, too great to count, from every nation and tribe and people and language" (Revelation 7:9).

In our understanding, to choose one thing automatically excludes others. When my children had birthday parties, I allowed them to invite only a small number of children. I find large numbers of small children in confined spaces a bad idea. My children had to choose some of their friends and exclude others, but God isn't like me! He chooses the Israelites as the first ones to become his children (Jeremiah 2:3), but not the only ones. God doesn't exclude others. Rather, he invites everyone to be part of his chosen people.

The Church

In the New Testament, the church is now God's chosen people, "You are a chosen people. You are royal priests, a holy nation, God's very own possession. As a result, you can show others the goodness of God" (1 Peter 2:9).

God didn't change his mind concerning Israel. Indeed, Paul writes at length explaining this isn't the case (Romans

9–11). However, a further unfolding of God's purposes occurs. Israel's disobedience becomes an opportunity for other nations to join with the Jewish faithful remnant to show the world how good it is to live according to his ways (11:11–12). When we accept Christ as our Lord and Savior, we're included in God's family, regardless of whether we're Jew or gentile. Together we are his chosen people.

> For he chose us in advance, and he makes everything work out according to his plan. … And now you Gentiles have also heard the truth, the Good News that God saves you. And when you believed in Christ, he identified you as his own by giving you the Holy Spirit. (Ephesians 1:11, 13)

Our Western, individualist mindset tends to apply the promise of being chosen to individuals. However, Paul writes his words to the church at Ephesus. We become chosen by exercising faith and becoming part of God's church—his body. So being chosen doesn't mean others are excluded. Instead, we desire to include others and pray for them to exercise faith so they, too, can become part of God's church.

God chooses us, his church, to bless the world.

One Task

Once we fulfill God's plan to become part of his church, what's next? Rather surprisingly, God has only one thing for us to do. There's just one thing on our to-do list, and it's only three words long:

Become like Jesus.

Christ gave us gifted leaders so "we all come to such unity in our faith and knowledge of God's Son that we will be mature in the Lord, measuring up to the full and complete standard of Christ" (Ephesians 4:13).

"We will speak the truth in love, growing in every way more and more like Christ, who is the head of his body, the church" (v. 15).

God plans to make us more and more like Christ.

Our abilities, our giftings, and our callings enable us to partake in the tasks God has for us. As we serve others, we're presented with numerous opportunities to grow more Christlike.

Gladys Aylward was a missionary in China for 20 years. She remarked, "I don't think I was God's first choice for what I've done in China. There was somebody else, a man perhaps. But for some reason he wouldn't go. He wouldn't answer God's call. Anyway, God looked down and saw me and said, 'Well, she's willing.'"[2]

Did God really have somebody else in mind to go to China? Or was Gladys having a bad day and feeling inadequate?

As I considered this, I happened across the story of Esther. I came to the part where Mordecai tells Esther about Haman's plot to kill all the Jews.

> "If you keep quiet at a time like this, deliverance and relief for the Jews will arise from some other place, but you and your relatives will die. Who knows if perhaps you were made queen for just such a time as this?" (Esther 4:14)

Mordecai is confident that if Esther doesn't go to the king and ask for mercy, God will send help another way. God presents Esther with the opportunity to save her people, but she could refuse. Even then, God would still save his people from annihilation. God's plans aren't thwarted by people's reluctance or disobedience.

Esther rises to the challenge and does indeed save her people. Will we rise to the challenge and use the opportunities we've been given to have an impact for Christ?

God's Projects

Paul tells us, "We are God's masterpiece. He has created us anew in Christ Jesus, so we can do the good things he planned for us long ago" (Ephesians 2:10).

We're God's masterpiece, his handiwork, his project.

Many of us have projects we're working on. For some, it's a patchwork quilt, a new garden bed, a renovated piece of furniture, or maybe a hobby—like completing a jigsaw.

It's something we plan to work on over time.

God's project is to make us like Jesus. That's a long-term project! God can achieve his purposes in many ways, so there's a great variety of things we could do. We never have to worry about people or circumstances stealing God's plan for our life—or worrying about making the wrong life choices—because his primary plan is to make us like Jesus. This continues regardless of our vocation or our situation in life.

Often the places God asks us to serve aren't what we imagine. They don't feel like a natural fit for us because God pushes us out of our comfort zones to grow us so we become more Christlike.

Becoming Christlike

Most people in the Bible seem unqualified for the tasks God assigns to them. Amos is an Old Testament prophet from Tekoa, a small mountain village south of Jerusalem. He lives shortly after Jonah. He's a shepherd when God calls him to prophesy. Amos clarifies.

> I'm not a professional prophet, and I was never trained to be one. I'm just a shepherd, and I take care of sycamore-fig trees. But the Lord called me away from my flock and told me, "Go and prophesy to my people in Israel." (Amos 7:14–15)

Amos has a tough job. None of the kings of Israel follow God's ways, so Amos's messages aren't well received.

Archaeological digs confirm that Israel is enjoying a time of prosperity, but the poor are oppressed and denied justice.[3] There's rampant immorality and drunkenness (2:6–8).

The people have no interest in Amos's warnings about God's judgments. They don't repent and are eventually taken captive and sent into exile. Amos could give God a lot of good reasons not to prophesy to Israel, and perhaps he even thinks he isn't God's first choice.

- He doesn't have the right background or training to be a prophet.

- He's from "the hills," and not from Jerusalem, the center of public worship at the temple.

- The Israelites won't listen.

Still, nowhere do we see Amos complaining or running in the other direction like Jonah. He's faithful in the task that God gives him to do. He doesn't get a lot of applause, not then and not now.

Amos is a quiet achiever.

I relate to Amos and find his story a great encouragement. He carries out God's task for him, even though it's not a natural fit, and he doesn't experience a lot of success. Yet in the process, Amos grows in godliness.

Sometimes, I sense God asking me to do things, like public speaking, that don't come naturally to me. Once I told God I was never going to speak in public again. I refused all invitations to speak, which often came my way simply because I was the pastor's wife. I even managed to persuade Ross to tell interview boards for future positions that I don't speak to groups.

Then one day, I sensed God's conviction to stop telling people that I don't speak in public. "That's fine," I thought. The church I attended had stopped asking, and we were already known to the people at our next church. They knew not to ask. I thought I was safe.

However, when we moved to Corryong (which I explain in Chapter 2), I was so amazed at the way God orchestrated events, I wanted to tell everyone. Slowly and gradually, I found I had other things I wanted to share. I received positive feedback from my devotional thoughts, and Ross encouraged me to share my thoughts with a larger audience. I began volunteering to speak, even when I was sure others would do a better job.

As I began to speak in public, I found my trust in God grew and I could overcome my fears and experience his enabling. In the process, I became a little more Christlike.

God's enabling is enough for any task.

Flexible Plans

Not only are God's tasks surprising, but so are his methods. Studying the Gospels, we find Jesus has no standard operating procedure. If he's asked to come and heal a sick child, sometimes he goes, as in the case of Jairus (Luke 8:41–42), but sometimes he doesn't, as with the official's son (John 4:46–54). Sometimes he lays hands on the sick person, and sometimes he doesn't. Jesus doesn't have a set pattern, and once, he even hesitates.

Why would Jesus hesitate before he helps?

Jesus is in Tyre and Sidon when a Canaanite woman asks him to help her suffering daughter. After initially not responding at all, Jesus says, "I was sent only to help God's lost sheep—the people of Israel" (Matthew 15:24).

This is odd since he has already healed the Roman centurion's servant, even offering to go to his house (Luke 7:6). Jesus does eventually heal the woman's daughter, but why the hesitation?

Perhaps the best explanation is found in his own words, "I will do what the Father requires of me" (John 14:31). Jesus isn't following a predetermined blueprint, but he's listening to his Father. "The Son can do nothing by himself. He does only what he sees the Father doing. Whatever the Father does, the Son also does" (5:19).

Jesus's flexibility teaches us an important truth. God's tasks are tailor-made for each situation. We can't assume God will always do the same thing in the same way. God may have worked a particular way in my life or in the lives of the people I know, but this doesn't permit me to insist that God work in that way in other people's lives. Sometimes, I've acted like I know the best thing to do in a situation and freely given others advice.

These days, I pause when asked for advice and quickly pray for God's wisdom rather than thrusting my good intentions upon them.

Detours

Detours are also a natural part of life when you follow God. The apostle Paul intends to go to Asia to preach the gospel, but one night he has a vision of a man from Macedonia begging him to come over and help them (Acts

16:6–9). So Paul travels to Macedonia and spends time in three towns: Philippi, Thessalonica, and Berea. Paul is forced to leave all three places. In Philippi, Paul and his traveling companion Silas are thrown into jail (vv. 37–39). In Thessalonica, there's a riot (17:5), and in Berea, Paul hurries away to avoid more trouble (vv. 13–14).

We tend to expect if God sends us on a mission, it will be successful. We don't expect to be driven out of town. I wonder if Paul ever doubted his guidance:

"God, did you really send me here?"

However, there are many positive results. Lydia responds to God, and a church starts in Philippi. A slave girl finds freedom from the devil's power. A jailer and his family repent (Acts 16). In Thessalonica, some Jews and a large number of Greeks come to believe that Jesus is the Christ. The Bereans study the Scriptures with great eagerness, and again many Jews and Greeks believe (17:1–15). Paul's work in Macedonia has far-reaching effects, and today we have the blessings of Paul's letters to the Philippians and the Thessalonians.

We don't always see the fruit of our efforts at the time. Sometimes God sends us into troubled situations, and we may be forced to leave before we've finished the job. Others may be called to spend a long time in one place, with little evidence of any growth. Either way, God's purposes aren't thwarted. His Spirit continues to work in the lives of people whether we remain or not.

The idea that God has wildly different expectations of his children can be mystifying. When I spend time with parents of young children, I find they have similar hopes for all of their children. They would like their children to be productively employed in a worthwhile pursuit. God wants the same thing for his children, but his definitions of "productive" and "worthwhile" differ from ours. We tend to look at achievements in worldly terms, while God looks at them spiritually.

The writer to the Hebrews encourages us to "strip off every weight that slows us down, especially the sin that so easily trips us up. And let us run with endurance the race God has set before us" (Hebrews 12:1).

We run our race and not someone else's.

Finding the Race God Has for Us

God hasn't left us without direction. When the early church wrestles with the issue of how to include the gentiles in their fellowship, they base their decision on three criteria:

- The way God is already leading them (Acts 15:14–15).

- Evidence from Peter, Paul, and Barnabas on how God works in the lives of the gentiles (vv. 6–12).

- Scripture—James quotes Amos 9:11–12 in reference to the gentiles (vv. 16–18).

Their decision also comes with a sense of peace, "it seemed good to the Holy Spirit and to us" (v. 28).

In my own life when seeking God's direction, I find it helpful to think about how God has already been working in my life. What areas has God been encouraging me in? What Bible verses have stood out to me lately? What songs have spoken to me? What do I enjoy? God plants desires in me that he intends for me to pursue.

Still, the time will come to step out in faith, believing that God is guiding, and then trusting him with the outcome. We can expect to have a sense of peace about such decisions because they fit so well with what he has already shown us.

The Amplified Bible explains this peace particularly well. "Let the peace (soul harmony which comes) from Christ rule (act as umpire continually) in your hearts [deciding and settling with finality all questions that arise in your minds]" (Colossians 3:15 AMPC).

Nevertheless, it can be daunting, so it's good to remember that God is always with us, even if our plans fail.

Do God's Plans Fail?

God's plans won't fail. Revelation 21–22 describe their glorious fulfillment. Nevertheless, sometimes completing the tasks God has for us isn't as effective as we expect. Missionaries, chaplains, and other mission workers spend years building their credibility and relationships with their community. They may never see the results of their efforts. To focus solely on the immediate results of our ministry can be shortsighted.

God calls Isaiah to preach to his people but tells him they won't listen. The cities will lay in ruins because of their disobedience (Isaiah 6:9–13). Isaiah preaches for forty years to unresponsive people. Perhaps God tells him in advance so he doesn't focus on the results. Isaiah's apparent lack of short-term success is important in the larger scheme of God's purposes since he gives everyone the opportunity to repent.

Likewise, Jeremiah preaches for twenty-three years to people who don't listen (Jeremiah 25:3–4). Did Jeremiah and Isaiah worry about their lack of success? Many times, Jeremiah writes about his frustrations (9:2; 12:4; 15:10, 15–18; 20:7–10, 14–18). From a kingdom perspective, we hold these men in high regard since they make a huge contribution to the Old Testament books.

We, too, endeavor to complete the tasks God has for us and leave the results to him.

God Can Explain

When my children were teenagers, they would sometimes come home late from an event, or I would discover they hadn't completed a chore they said they would do. Before I had a chance to express my annoyance, they would say to me, "I can explain everything." Sometimes, they were able to provide a satisfactory explanation. Other times, not so much. As they grew older, their explanations became more authentic, and I became more confident they could indeed explain.

> One day, God will explain everything,
> or maybe it will be obvious.

Either way, I know God has the capacity to offer me a completely satisfactory explanation for everything that has happened in my life, my community, and my world. Don't let the devil steal your confidence in God's ability to bring about his plans in his timing.

God's plans aren't the domineering strategies of a dictator, or the muddled impulses of a mystic, or the maneuvered strategies of a master chess player. Rather his plans are an intricate tapestry where every stitch adds to the design. They're an adventure story with dangers and difficulties. They're a multithousand-piece jigsaw puzzle that leaves us with ambiguity and mystery until the final piece is put in place. One day, all the pieces will finally come together and make perfect sense. One day we'll see the whole panorama of God's plans.

I have confidence in following God's guidance because I know his ultimate aim is to make me more like Christ, and while that's a challenge, it's a plan that's good for me and my world.

Let's Pray

Thank you, Lord, that your plans are good. They're inclusive plans to bless all people. Thank you, Lord, that as a believer, I'm part of your church—your chosen instrument to bless the world.

Thank you, too, for not having a long list of things for me to do in my lifetime. Thank you that I can't miss your plan because you can use all the circumstances and situations in my life to make me more like you.

Empower me and grow me when you ask me to fulfill a role that is outside my natural tendencies and looks different from what I expect. Remind me that you will strengthen, equip, and enable me.

Ultimately, give me the faith to leave the successes or failures with you.

In Jesus's name.

Amen.

8

God Blesses

I have an acquaintance who's a professional gardener, but he doesn't like roses. How can anyone not like roses? Apparently, it's possible! He and his wife bought a property with an overgrown garden. He decided to pull out the entire garden and start from scratch. In among the tangle of plants and weeds, he was surprised to find the one and only type of rose he did like, a particular variety of climbing rose. I thought, "Wow, isn't God gracious?" But I said nothing. I've discovered that not everyone sees God's blessings operating like this, and for a long time, neither did I.

As I listen to Christians, I find that some have very specific ideas about what God should and shouldn't do in their lives, from giving a good medical report, to converting kids, to supplying finances, to finding a space in a crowded parking lot. These expectations often get in the way of recognizing God's goodness to us.

Does God really bless his children?

There's much evidence to suggest he doesn't. God's people seem to have their share of health issues, financial difficulties, and relationship dramas. The older brother in the story of the prodigal son complains to his father, "You never gave me even one young goat for a feast with my friends" (Luke 15:29).

Perhaps we feel the same. We may have lived a good moral life, regularly attended church, and helped those in distress yet feel like God hasn't blessed us with even a goat—though I'm not sure what I would do with a goat!

Yet the truth is God has indeed blessed us, and not barely but lavishly. "He is so rich in kindness and grace that he purchased our freedom with the blood of his Son and forgave our sins. He has showered his kindness on us, along with all wisdom and understanding" (Ephesians 1:7–8).

God isn't miserly. He showers his grace in abundance. If God gave us nothing else except forgiveness, that would be enough to warrant our eternal gratitude. Yet he gives us so much more.

God blesses us—first with salvation, but also in other ways, unexpectedly, undeservedly, lavishly.

God touches our lives with unmerited blessings, not always the ones we hoped for, but blessings nevertheless. There's an abundance of God's blessings available, but are we open to receiving all that God has for us?

Let God love you

When I worked in libraries, I enjoyed returning the books to the shelves. This provided me with the opportunity to see what books were being borrowed and what books the library stocked. One day, I noticed a book called *Receiving Love: Transform Your Relationship by Letting Yourself Be Loved*.[1] This isn't a Christian book, but the title struck me, particularly the phrase "letting yourself be loved."

During the time I struggled emotionally following Ross's cancer diagnosis, God graciously sent some people into my life to help me. After chatting with one of these people, I sensed God speaking to me.

"Let me love you."

I was seriously challenged. I suddenly became aware that I was keeping God at arm's length and he wasn't happy about this arrangement.

I remembered Revelation 3:20: "Look! I stand at the door and knock. If you hear my voice and open the door, I will come in, and we will share a meal together as friends."

This verse occurs in the letter to the church at Laodicea. That is, it's written to Christians. God still knocks at the door of our hearts, wanting a deeper relationship with us. God was waiting for me to open the door of my heart a little wider to receive from him.

He wasn't going to force his way past the barriers I had erected around my heart. Over the next few months, I started to learn how to take the barriers down so I could receive God's blessings.

Consequently, when I read the words on the cover of the library book, "letting yourself be loved," I thought I might glean something from the book. I took it home and started flipping through it. The authors' premise isn't that people ought to find better ways of showing love to their spouses and partners but rather that people need to learn how to receive the love that's already being offered to them.

Is this true? I began thinking about the relationships in my own life, with Ross and with God. I thought about the many things Ross does for me. Often, he will cook dinner, do the dishes, or do a load of laundry, but I might barely acknowledge it. I wondered why this was so. I was forced to acknowledge I wasn't a good receiver.

Receiving

Jesus teaches, "Do to others as you would like them to do to you" (Luke 6:31).

Yet people's preferred ways of showing kindness may be very different from mine. Someone might give me some homegrown produce, an indoor plant, or a book that I "must read." People show kindness according to their own inclinations. So I learned to receive their acts of kindness with gratitude for their thoughtfulness, even if I wasn't particularly grateful for the actual gift.

I had a lot of unhealthy expectations around how people ought to show me kindness. These days, I take more notice of the way my family and friends show me consideration and understanding. I express my thankfulness, even when their actions aren't my first preference. I'm on a learning curve.

Often I prefer to be the one giving the blessing rather than receiving it. Yet if I don't learn how to become a good receiver, I deprive others of the blessing of giving.

Compliments, gifts, and expressions of appreciation can leave me feeling uncomfortable instead of blessed. Somehow, being on the receiving end stirs a mixture of emotions in me. Sometimes I feel unworthy, indebted, inadequate, incompetent, or dependent. Receiving requires a certain openness, humility, and vulnerability on my part.

I find it difficult to be a gracious receiver. I expect if someone blesses me, I will feel happy about it. I'm better at receiving when it concerns the big issues in my life, things I know I can't handle on my own.

Yet God also teaches us to be good receivers in the everyday little things—a hug, a cup of tea, a short text of thanks, a simple meal. Jesus encourages us to pray, "Give us each day the food we need" (Luke 11:3).

As I read the Gospels, I notice Jesus is good at receiving from God and others. At his baptism, Jesus receives the gift of the Spirit and his Father's affirmation (Mark 1:9–11). He also receives from others. He accepts the physical anointing from the woman with the alabaster jar of perfume (Luke 7:37–38), which may have been somewhat embarrassing as the woman steps outside social conventions to bless him. He accepts a leper's thankfulness (Luke 17:16) and the help of angels (Matthew 4:11). Jesus is our example of a good receiver.

God Blesses

God intends for us to grow in our ability to receive his acceptance, affirmation, and assistance and not to be like the unwilling people of Jerusalem. "How often I have wanted to gather your children together as a hen protects her chicks beneath her wings, but you wouldn't let me" (Luke 13:34). Instead, God desires for us to act like little children, who accept gifts enthusiastically, without reservation or thought of reciprocating.

Some won't receive from God. How sad.

God wants to bless us, but often we miss his blessings because they aren't what we expect or even want. His blessings come in many ways—through the beauty of nature, through others, or through amazing coincidences—like finding the one and only rose you like growing unexpectedly in your garden.

One Saturday morning, two of my adult children had to drive through the small town where I live to attend a football game in the city. Since others were going to the match, they decided to rendezvous in our town at the only gas station. They were going to be in my town for only five minutes and didn't bother to tell me they were stopping. However, as it happened, I needed to go to the supermarket that morning and Ross needed gas. Consequently, we accidentally met our children at the gas station and five minutes quickly became ten.

God and parents know, but children not quite so much, that there's nothing like seeing someone face-to-face. Phone calls, emails, texts, and even video calls aren't the same as physical meetings. You lose all the inflection when communication is written down, plus you lose all the body language when you can't see someone. And even when you can see someone electronically, hugging the computer won't give you a sense of their presence. So, God arranged a little face-to-face meeting with my kids to bless my heart.

Be on the lookout for blessings only God can provide.

Honors

God not only blesses us with special roses and impromptu

meetings but may even publicly honor or reward us. Annually in Australia, on Australia Day people are honored for their public service, contributions to society, or outstanding deeds. Schools honor highly successful children at end of the year graduations. Likewise, God may choose to honor his children.

> How great is the goodness
> you have stored up for those who fear you.
> You lavish it on those who come to you
> for protection,
> blessing them before the watching world.
> (Psalm 31:19)

There's an interesting incident in the book of Esther when the king realizes he hasn't rewarded Mordecai for saving him from an assassination attempt. He asks, "What should I do to honor a man who truly pleases me?" (Esther 6:6).

Likewise, there are times when God, our King, delights to honor his people. We might see God pouring out his blessing on a particular person or a church. In pastoral ministry, I've seen God bless churches, but not necessarily the one I'm attending. What's my response?

What has been your response when God blesses others? Are we angry, like the elder brother? Do we bemoan our lack of a goat? Or do we rejoice with those who rejoice? Even when they get a blessing we would have liked?

Interestingly, it's often easier to mourn with those who mourn than to rejoice with those God has chosen to honor. God is sovereign. He can bless anyone he wants with whatever sort of blessing he chooses. Our response will be one of gratitude when we understand we have a God who delights to bless his people.

Ask

To receive God's blessings, we ask. Theologian Craig Blomberg writes about the parable of the unjust judge in Luke 18:1–8, "There are good things God desires his people to have but which he has determined to give them only if they seek him in prayer." [2]

An example of this is Jabez's prayer in the Old Testament. His prayer starts with the words, "Oh, that you would bless me." At the end, "God granted him his request" (1 Chronicles 4:10).

Jabez has no problem asking God to bless him, but sometimes I do. I may not ask because I believe I can make it on my own, I don't need anyone's help, or I'm unworthy of people's time and effort. When I feel this way, pride blocks God's blessings. When I'm humble enough to ask God for what I need, I find him not only meeting my needs but providing other blessings as well.

I've found I can ask God about anything, even the weather.

While Jesus is teaching his disciples about the timing of future events, he includes this directive: "And pray that your flight will not be in winter" (Mark 13:18).

Regardless of whether this particular instruction is about the destruction of Jerusalem in AD 70 or to an event still to take place, it remains informative. Jesus doesn't say pray this won't happen. He says pray this won't take place in winter. In context, if one needs to flee the city, it would be better if weather conditions are mild.

While God is sovereign and runs the world according to his agenda, our prayers do have an effect. Our prayers can rearrange events to our advantage. The verse teaches us that God cares about every aspect of our problems, even the weather. When bad things happen, we can still pray that God will minimize the difficulties and bring about better than expected outcomes.

We may wonder why Jesus doesn't ask us to pray that God's people will be spared hardship. Suffering isn't an easy thing to accept when we know God is powerful enough to prevent it. However, God has something bigger in mind than for us to live trouble-free lives. In the long term, God is making a new heaven and a new earth. While we wait for this day, we can pray for good outcomes.

Our prayers do impact circumstances.

Meanwhile, James teaches us that sometimes the reason we don't receive the answers we want is because of our motives. "You don't have what you want because you don't ask God for it. And even when you ask, you don't get it because your motives are all wrong—you want only what will give you pleasure" (James 4:2–3).

We can become better candidates for God's blessings by examining our motives. In the Beatitudes, Jesus teaches us eight attitudes we can adopt to become better receivers of God's blessings.

Becoming Good Receivers

I remember when the song *Show Me Your Ways* by

Darlene Zschech was first released in 1996. At the time I wondered why some Christians seemed to live more blessed lives than others. I didn't only sing *Show Me Your Ways*. I prayed it. God directed my attention to the godly attitudes found in the Beatitudes. I've also included opposing attitudes that steal our blessings.

- **"God blesses those who are poor and realize their need for him" (Matthew 5:3).** Being spiritually poor means acknowledging that I need help from God and other people. We're dependent on God's mercy and forgiveness. We can do nothing to earn God's mercy, nor can we in any way pay God back. The attitudes that steal are pride and independence.

- **"God blesses those who mourn, for they will be comforted" (v. 4).** The prerequisite to receiving God's comfort is that we mourn. If we don't mourn and admit our pain and loss, we cannot receive God's comfort. So we allow ourselves to feel our emotional pains. The attitude that steals is being in denial about our heartaches.

- **"God blesses those who are humble" (v. 5).** Humility is the characteristic of being submissive and not demanding our own way. A humble attitude shows itself by accepting God's agenda and his timetable. The attitude that steals is seeking to control a situation for our own advantage.

- **"God blesses those who hunger and thirst for justice" (v. 6).** Justice or righteousness (NIV) in this context refers to personal holiness and faithfulness to God and his will.[3] This blessing comes to those who are passionate about following God's ways in their own life and for revival in their community. The attitude that steals is having a casual attitude toward our walk with God.

- **"God blesses those who are merciful" (v. 7).** You can show mercy only if you've been hurt by someone. The merciful are people who acknowledge the damage done by another and extend forgiveness to that person. The attitude that steals is expecting people to toughen up and simply get over their pain. Forgiveness is a huge topic, but keep in mind that no matter how badly we've been hurt by someone, it's still not as great as our offenses against a holy God. His holiness is so immense, that other people's offenses are modest in comparison. Another helpful thought is to find a reason to forgive. Jesus prays for the soldiers who crucify him, "Father, forgive them, for they don't know what they are doing" (Luke 23:34). Often, those who hurt us, don't realize the impact of their actions. God's blessing comes to those who cultivate a forgiving attitude toward others.

- **"God blesses those whose hearts are pure" (Matthew 5:8).** The prophet Malachi describes

Jesus as "a blazing fire that refines metal, or like a strong soap that bleaches clothes" (Malachi 3:2). His ministry has a purifying effect (v. 3). Jesus achieves this by using people and circumstances in our lives to reveal and refine our attitudes. David wants a pure heart, so he prays, "Search me, O God, and know my heart; test me and know my anxious thoughts" (Psalm 139:23). The blessing of God comes to those who are prepared to deal with their inner attitudes and motives and thus become pure in heart. The attitudes that steal are cover-ups and deception to create a good impression.

- **"God blesses those who work for peace" (Matthew 5:9).** Peacemakers are not peace-at-any-price people but those who are determined to rebuild a relationship that has been damaged. Paul instructs us, "Do all that you can to live in peace with everyone" (Romans 12:18). Sometimes, even after we've done all we can, peace isn't possible, but if the other person is willing, a peacemaker will make every effort to restore a relationship. The attitude that steals is whitewashing problems and not taking seriously their impact on others.

- **"God blesses those who are persecuted for doing right" (Matthew 5:10).** Persecution comes in many forms, not just physical abuse. If we want God's blessing on our lives, we need to press on despite misunderstandings, false accusations, and lack of support or interest, even from those who are important in our lives. The attitudes that steal are yielding to peer pressure or conceding when facing difficult circumstances.

Receiving God's blessings means being prepared to work on our motives and cultivate Christlike attitudes.

Although, we can't assume God's blessing indicates his approval.

Blessing Disobedience?

Moses disobeys God in the desert at Kadesh when he strikes the rock with his staff. Yet "water gushed out. So the entire community and their livestock drank their fill" (Numbers 20:11).

God tells Moses to speak to the rock, not strike it. Nevertheless, God blesses the community by providing water. We may find it confusing when God blesses someone despite their disobedience.

The sailors who throw Jonah overboard have an encounter with God. An encounter they wouldn't have had if Jonah had obeyed God and gone to Nineveh in the first place (Jonah 1:16).

How do we explain a God who blesses when there has been obvious disobedience?

We see it in our day when a prominent Christian is exposed for being involved in immorality, fraud, or mismanagement. Often, it turns out that the situation has been going on for some time and during that same period people have been blessed by the person's ministry. How do we understand that?

These incidents speak of the enormity of God's kindness and patience toward us. God waits for the person to repent before publicly revealing their sin. If they don't repent, God cannot let it continue, and he will eventually allow them to be exposed.

We can't assume God's patience gives us a license for sin (Jude v. 4 NIV). If we become involved in activities we know aren't honoring to God, we deny his presence in our lives, even though God may still bless our ministry. We cannot assume God's blessings mean he approves of our actions. Neither does an apparent lack of blessing mean he disapproves.

God doesn't allow Moses into the Promised Land—a reminder not to take God's patience for granted.

A Miracle

As we look back over our lives, we'll see God has blessed us, but perhaps not in the way we prayed for, hoped for, or expected. Yet ultimately in ways God deemed best for us.

As I review my life, I can see I'm a different person from the shy teenager who gave her life to Christ fifty years ago. My life is a miracle. I'm doing things now I never dreamed possible—like writing books and speaking in public. This wasn't an instant miracle but a slow journey with many highs and lows as I learned to trust God and receive from him.

God is more willing to bless us than we're willing to

receive. We want God to bless us so our lives are easier, more comfortable, and less stressful. But God is more interested in our growth toward holiness than in our temporary comfort.

He blesses us so we can be a blessing to others.

His blessings enable and encourage us to reach out to others. With the benefit of hindsight, we'll see that through receiving his Spirit, his enabling, and his endurance, our lives are miracles because we couldn't have become the person we are now in our own strength.

David assures us that God's goodness will pursue us (Psalm 23:6), but will we have eyes to see it? The starry expanse of God's creativity is there all the time, even though we see it only at night. In the same way, God's blessings are always there to receive, if we're willing.

Let's Pray

Thank you, Lord, that you do indeed bless me more than I realize. Open my eyes to see the many blessings I already have in you. May I be attentive to those interventions only you could have orchestrated.

As I seek to apply the Beatitudes to my life, teach me, and enable me to change my attitude so I become a better recipient of your blessings. Bring to my attention any areas where I am hindering your blessings from impacting my life and help me be a good receiver.

Give me the wisdom and courage to be childlike and unafraid to ask for your blessings and also for the generosity to share them with others.

Thank you that my life is a miracle because of what you have done and continue to do in my life.

In Jesus's name.

Amen.

9

God Gives Peace

One night, I waited for Ross to come home from visiting someone in the hospital. We were living in an isolated community with no mobile phone coverage. At about the time I expected him home, I looked out our lounge room window and over the paddocks. I saw flashing lights and signs of an accident on the road that led to our house. Traffic was backed up and unable to pass. I had no way of knowing if Ross was in the traffic waiting to pass or whether he was involved in the accident. I desperately wanted to jump in my car to see if Ross was alright. However, I had three small children asleep in their beds, and there was nothing I could do but wait ... and wait ... and wait.

When my attention was on the flashing lights, my mind was anxious and filled with negative scenarios. But when I focused on God, I felt a sense of peace.

I spent the evening fluctuating between looking at the flashing lights and focusing on God. The air ambulance came, but it took a long time before it finally lifted off and traffic was allowed to pass. I was extremely relieved when Ross made it home.

God desires to give us peace. However, if our minds focus on the "flashing lights," on our worries and fears, we won't be able to live in peace. Peace comes from resting in our relationship with God.

> Jesus said, "Come to me, all of you who are weary and carry heavy burdens, and I will give you rest. Take my yoke upon you. Let me teach you, because I am humble and gentle at heart, and you will find rest for your souls." (Matthew 11:28–29)

These verses speak of two rests. The first rest is a gift we receive when we believe in Jesus as our Lord and Savior. The second rest we "find," as we learn from him, as we learn to trust God more deeply, learn his ways of doing things, and learn to keep in step with his Spirit.[1]

**God wants me to rest in him,
so he can give me peace.**

God's peace is inexplicable, comforting, and restorative. To experience this peace, we put our trust in God. This is easy to do when our lives are running smoothly—difficult when they aren't. But when our lives aren't running smoothly, that's the time we most need his peace.

Rest for My Soul

I've met some people in churches who have a negative view of God, as if he's never satisfied, like a cruel slave driver or a demanding taskmaster. This view puzzles me because God encourages his people to rest. In the Old Testament, God instigates many festivals so the Israelites can take time off and celebrate his goodness. A couple of these festivals last seven days. He also ordains the seventh day of the week as a Sabbath, when his people are to refrain from work. Furthermore, he insists they observe it.

For example, when God emphasizes the blessings that would follow obedience, he picks two of the commandments. "Do not make idols or set up carved images, or sacred pillars, or sculptured stones in your land so you may worship them. I am the Lord your God. You must keep my Sabbath days of rest" (Leviticus 26:1–2).

Why does God highlight these two commandments?

Not only is worshiping idols pointless, but it also places people in the position of trying to earn divine approval. Whereas God tells his people they already have his approval (Deuteronomy 7:6). He wants them to feel worthwhile and valued because they're his chosen people, not because they have performed a religious activity.

Second, God gives them the Sabbath as a gift to remind his people they depend on his provision, not on the work of their hands. Every week, on the Sabbath, God reminds them their relationship with him isn't maintained by their works.

These two things would help God's people enjoy his peace, and they are still important, even though we experience them differently under the new covenant. Today, not worshiping idols means having nothing in our lives that's more important to us than God. Having no other sense of identity except being a child of God. Keeping the Sabbath means acknowledging we cannot achieve salvation by our works but rely on God's provision of a Savior.

These days, I've found few people who are concerned

about taking a day to rest. When keeping the Sabbath is mentioned, it seems to be in the context of catching up on sleep because they've been so busy the rest of the week. This is a long way from God's intention of reminding us that we depend on him and not on our achievements.

Jesus brought a new covenant understanding of the role of the Sabbath. "There remains, then, a Sabbath-rest for the people of God; for anyone who enters God's rest also rests from their works, just as God did from his" (Hebrews 4:9–10 NIV).

God wants our souls to rest in him. He encourages us to rest and remind ourselves of his provision. However, like the Israelites of old, we're often reluctant to fully rest in God.

A Good King

To rest in God requires confidence that a good God is looking after us. An evil king isn't interested in stopping strife, but a good king wants his people to live in peace. God is the ultimate good king, and even when our circumstances aren't peaceful, he wants us to know his peace in our hearts. Gideon is the first person to refer to God as the God of peace.

In Gideon's day, Israel doesn't have a king or a military leader. Instead, God calls individuals to lead the Israelites against local enemies as the need arises. At this time, the Midianites are overpowering the Israelites so they can't even harvest their crops (Judges 6:3–4).

After seven years of conflict (v. 1), the angel of the Lord appears to Gideon. He tells Gideon that God is sending him to deliver the Israelites from the Midianites. Gideon finds this unlikely and asks two questions.

First he asks, "If the Lord is with us, why has all this happened to us?" (v. 13).

This question has been with us for a long time. The book of Job is thought to be one of the oldest books in the Bible,[2] and Job wants to know why so many disasters happened to him. Job never gets an explanation, but he does get God's presence, and in the end, that is enough. We won't always know the answer to the "why" question, but we can be assured of God's presence.

Then there's the "how" question. "How can I rescue Israel? My clan is the weakest in the whole tribe of Manasseh, and I am the least in my entire family!" (v. 15).

How can I make a difference? I'm an insignificant person in my community, my church, and my family. What can I do?

The Lord answers, "I will be with you. And you will destroy the Midianites as if you were fighting against one man" (v. 16).

We make a difference because God is with us.

The answer to both the "why" question and the "how" question turns out to be the same, God's presence. God is with us, not only to hold our hands when things get difficult but also to empower us. God says to Gideon, "Mighty hero, the Lord is with you!" (v. 12).

Gideon certainly doesn't feel like a mighty hero, but that's how God sees him, and he eventually becomes a hero. When we believe God's truth, it changes us.

Shalom

Gideon's encounter with God continues. He rushes home to prepare an offering which he places before the angel. It's consumed by fire (vv. 17–21).

> When Gideon realized that it was the angel of the Lord, he cried out, "Oh, Sovereign Lord, I'm doomed! I have seen the angel of the Lord face to face!"
> "It is all right," the Lord replied. "Do not be afraid. You will not die." And Gideon built an altar to the Lord there and named it Yahweh-Shalom (which means "the Lord is peace"). (Judges 6:22–24)

Gideon doesn't call God "The Lord is peace" because his circumstances have suddenly been resolved. God hasn't stepped in and miraculously defeated the enemy. At this point, the Midianites are still alive and well. Gideon calls the Lord "peace" because he learns that God is our peace regardless of our situation.

By resting in God's provision and holding on to peace in difficult times, we demonstrate our trust in God. It becomes obvious to the spiritual forces that oppose us that the peace we're experiencing comes from God and not our circumstances. This strikes a decisive blow to the enemy of our souls. We demonstrate our belief in something greater and more enduring than temporary relief from our problems. We believe God is doing a work that has eternal consequences.

If we allow ourselves to become agitated and disturbed by life events, we give the devil a foothold. Our minds won't remain peaceful if we dwell on potential bad outcomes.

How do we hold on to our peace when our circumstances aren't peaceful?

Stay Calm

I once worked with a colleague who wouldn't kill a fly for fear of upsetting her karma. I thought it sad her sense of peace was so fragile, but this is the only peace the world can offer—a precarious peace that requires constant effort to avoid conflict. Whereas God gives peace as a gift to those who rest in him. We don't have to avoid difficult situations or difficult people but rather be good receivers. Jesus said, "I am leaving you with a gift—peace of mind and heart. And the peace I give is a gift the world cannot give" (John 14:27).

Paul instructs us to "Stay calm" (1 Thessalonians 4:11 MSG). But how do we stay calm in a crisis? How do we stay calm when everyone around us is upset?

To fully enter God's rest and be at peace, we need to be deeply convinced that God is sovereign. We stay calm by believing God is in control and nothing can happen without his knowledge or permission. God is with me, enabling and sustaining me, so I focus on the thought that nothing can happen to me that I can't handle. We trust him to bring about good outcomes.

God's sovereignty is never under threat, so we can experience peace.

Even when people fail him, God's sovereignty isn't thwarted. Throughout the Old Testament, story after story shows us that Israel's disobedience didn't stop God fulfilling his purposes. And even through disappointing behavior, some still see the value of committing to God's ways (Ruth 1:18-21).

When we look through the Old Testament, we see many prophecies pointing to Jesus (Isaiah 9:6–7, Psalm 89:35–37). These prophecies remind us that God can bring about his purposes, regardless of the opposition. He has always been in charge and always will be. God knew we needed a Savior long before we did, and he has directed all the circumstances that led to Jesus dying for us. As we remember what God has done in the past, we know a good king is looking after us. This gives us confidence to trust him for the future.

God's Goodness

Is God a good king? Is he really good? This is the question at stake in the first temptation. The serpent suggests to Eve that if God were good, he wouldn't stop them from eating the fruit of the tree of the knowledge of good and evil. This is a lie that the devil has repeated again and again. If God is good, he won't keep good things from us (Genesis 3:5).

However, parents keep good things from their children. As a parent, I didn't give my children everything they asked for, nor did I allow them to do everything they wanted. I didn't buy my children every toy and every snack they liked, even if they were educational toys and healthy snacks. Sometimes saying no is the best thing a parent can do. Likewise, a good God will sometimes keep good things from us because he knows the long-term outcomes and has our best interests at heart.

If we complain that God is keeping things from us, we're saying God isn't looking after us and doesn't know what's best for us. We're saying our relationship with God isn't enough to satisfy us. We want more.

Yet God gives us so much—forgiveness, hope, eternal life, and peace.

At the cross, God demonstrates that he is a good God. He allows his only Son to be nailed to a cross, to take upon himself the punishment we deserve. A God who would voluntarily sacrifice himself to restore a relationship with us must have good intentions. At the cross, we see the character of God and his provision for us.

Peace Stealers

Fear and worry steal our peace. We can't be simultaneously fearful and peaceful. The knowledge that God loves us will calm our fears and give us peace. "He will take delight in you with gladness. With his love, he will calm all your fears. He will rejoice over you with joyful songs" (Zephaniah 3:17).

God is a loving Father who sees us as his beloved children. He longs for his children to come to him, trust his goodness, believe he rejoices over them, and allow his love to calm all their fears. Yet, we may not feel comfortable seeing God this way. Maybe we had a less-than-loving earthly father who has damaged our view of a father's love.

However, it would be a shame to let our past experiences prevent us from experiencing the love of our heavenly Father. We will find peace as we relax in the unmerited gift of God's rest.

Worrying also steals our peace. I once held the deluded belief that I achieved something by worrying. When I committed the situation to God, thoughts would bombard my mind, "If you stop worrying, it shows you don't care." Fortunately, I realized this is a lie of the devil.

Jesus asks, "Can all your worries add a single moment to your life?" (Luke 12:25).

Worrying achieves nothing, but it does rob us of peace.

I still find it a challenge not to be disturbed by circumstances and to remain at rest, but it's achievable. God wants to give me his peace, over and over again. I would prefer God rescue me from my troubles, but he hasn't promised me a stress-free life. Instead, we trust him to be our sustainer, giving us the wisdom and guidance to know what to do in any situation. He has promised us his presence, his strength, and his wisdom. He has also promised never to leave us or forsake us, and that's all we need.

The night I waited for Ross when I knew there had been an accident, I learned I could focus on God and experience his peace. I didn't find this easy, but I could do it. As I have practiced over the years focusing my thoughts on God's goodness, I've become quicker at noticing when my thoughts turn anxious. It's not effortless, but I've become better at it.

Thinking about the things God can do will encourage our faith. God can heal and restore, calm storms, make time stand still (Joshua 10:12–14), create everything or anything out of nothing (Colossians 1:15–16), and even restore the years the locusts have eaten away (Joel 2:25 NIV). He can also promote creative ideas. If we think something is a lost cause, it blocks our minds from seeking a positive outcome.

Being in Charge of Our Hearts

In some of Jesus's final words he gives the directive, "Don't let your hearts be troubled" (John 14:1) and shortly afterward adds, "So don't be troubled or afraid" (v. 27). Jesus gives us the responsibility of not allowing our hearts to be troubled or afraid. However, he doesn't leave us floundering. He instructs us how to have an untroubled heart: "Trust in God, and trust also in me" (v. 1).

The Amplified Bible is even more clear. "Stop allowing yourselves to be agitated and disturbed; and do not permit yourselves to be fearful and intimidated and cowardly and unsettled" (v. 27 AMPC).

Stop allowing myself ... Don't permit myself ... Clearly, it's up to me to control my emotions, but how?

Our emotions are connected to our thinking. Paul teaches us the importance of being careful about our thoughts. "Fix your thoughts on what is true, and honorable, and right, and pure, and lovely, and admirable. Think about things that are excellent and worthy of praise" (Philippians 4:8).

Choosing what we think about gives us control over our emotions and makes a huge difference to our emotional well-being. We cannot stop the doubts, the misgivings, and the "what ifs" from entering our minds, but we do have the choice of whether we continue to think about them. I can say to myself, "No, I'm not going to let my thoughts go down that path. I'm going to choose to trust God."

We can deliberately choose to focus on those things that are true—God is good, God is love, God is sovereign. Remember his promises.

Tearing Your Clothes

In the Old Testament, people tear their clothes when tragedy strikes. This is their way of expressing grief and distress. However, the high priest isn't allowed to tear his clothes (Leviticus 21:10). Furthermore, his clothes are made in such a way that would prevent even accidental tearing. "Reinforce the opening with a woven collar so it will not tear" (Exodus 28:32).

Today our High Priest is Jesus (Hebrews 4:14). Though he feels our pain, we can be confident that there's nothing Jesus would find so distressing that he would consider tearing his clothes. If our High Priest isn't feeling a sense of hopelessness, then there's no need for us to. Today, we're "royal priests" (1 Peter 2:9) following his priestly example. There's never a reason to become so overwhelmed when trouble or tragedy strikes that we would want to metaphorically tear our clothes.

God is in control. He isn't taken by surprise, and no problem is too hard for him. There is no need to despair. Nothing is too distressing because his help, his strengthening and enabling, is sufficient for any crisis. We can rest in his peace whatever the drama because we can approach God's throne at any time. "So let us come boldly to the throne of our gracious God. There we will receive his mercy, and we will find grace to help us when we need it most" (Hebrews 4:16).

Note well: God's help is supplied as needed, not in advance.

Oscar Thompson was an American pastor and professor. When he was diagnosed with cancer, he wrote in a letter to cancer patients, "God does not give dying grace on nondying days."[3] We can't stockpile his grace for emergencies. It's like the manna God gave the children of Israel. They had to collect it one day at a time and couldn't store it (Exodus 16:19–20). Likewise, we have to trust God to supply us with grace one day at a time. There's no point worrying about tomorrow's difficulties because God hasn't given us grace for that yet. "Today's trouble is enough for today" (Matthew 6:34). God supplies grace as we need it. And we will need it because Jesus promises difficulties.

Peace in Trouble

Jesus's disciples, like us, discover that his presence doesn't guarantee trouble-free circumstances. Jesus tells them, "Here on earth you will have many trials and sorrows" (John 16:33).

Are the disciples shocked to hear they will have trials?

After all, by this time they have seen Jesus perform many

miracles—turning water into wine, multiplying bread and fish, healing people, and raising others from the dead. Why would the disciples expect trouble when God could work miracles?

Immediately before this, Jesus said, "I have told you all this so that you may have peace in me" (v. 33).

In Jesus, we have peace, but not necessarily in our circumstances.

Elsewhere Paul writes, "Not that the troubles should come as any surprise to you. You've always known that we're in for this kind of thing. It's part of our calling. When we were with you, we made it quite clear that there was trouble ahead" (1 Thessalonians 3:3–4 MSG).

Paul teaches new believers to expect trouble—"it's part of our calling." The Christian life isn't about living in such a way as to avoid trouble but rather about having a strength that keeps us at peace despite what's happening in our lives. God could prevent difficulties, but he chooses to let us experience his peace in the midst of them.

Trouble is part of our calling.

If we give new believers the impression that their problems will be over when they become Christians, their faith may be destroyed when difficulties arise. Jesus explains this in the parable of the sower.

> The seed on the rocky soil represents those who hear the message and immediately receive it with joy. But since they don't have deep roots, they don't last long. They

fall away as soon as they have problems
or are persecuted for believing God's word.
(Matthew 13:20–21)

Our role model is Jesus, who taught us there will be toil, trials, and troubles, but as believers, we have the resources to cope. God has promised his power, his peace, and his presence to enable us to endure any difficulty.

The Lord gives his people strength.
　The Lord blesses them with peace. (Psalm 29:11)

Let's Pray

Thank you, Lord, for the gift of rest I received at salvation. Help me to learn from you so I can continue to find rest and peace for my soul.

Thank you, Lord, that nothing is so bad that it would cause me to metaphorically tear my clothes. I have no reason for despair because you're my High Priest. I always have access to your enabling grace.

When fearful and worrying thoughts drop uninvited into my mind, remind me to meditate on your unfailing love and faithfulness. Help me to focus on those things that will encourage my faith.

Thank you, Lord, that through your power, peace, and

presence you provide the resources I need to face the difficulties that come my way.

In Jesus's name.

Amen.

10

God Overcomes

One summer holiday, when my children were young, I had glandular fever. I spent a few weeks using the little energy I had to take my children to swimming lessons in the morning. Then, I'd come home and collapse on the couch.

The Australian tennis season was in full swing, and I watched a lot of tennis that summer. I fell into the Australian tradition of supporting the underdog. Usually, this was a young player competing against a more highly ranked opponent. I loved seeing them go for difficult shots, battling for every point, and not being intimidated. Most of these young players lost, but occasionally an experienced player took their opponent too lightly. This was a big mistake. The sheer determination of the younger player caught them by surprise, and they lost. I expect they learned not to treat the opposition flippantly in the future.

God, on the other hand, laughs at his opponents. He's never taken by surprise. "The one who rules in heaven laughs" (Psalm 2:4).

He laughs at the feeble efforts of his enemies. He knows any success his enemies experience is only temporary.

> The wicked plot against the godly;
> they snarl at them in defiance.

> But the Lord just laughs,
> for he sees their day of judgment coming.
> (Psalm 37:12–13)

God knows their ultimate defeat. The devil is on a limited time frame and can do nothing God doesn't allow. God laughs at those who attempt to thwart his purposes. This is a sign of his total disdain for the devil's plans. Evil won't win. The wicked won't have the final say.

God overcomes evil gloriously, victoriously, and jubilantly.

He knows that evil is only for a season, and time on earth is short compared to eternity.

The Devil's Strategy

While God laughs at his enemies, he never laughs at suffering. He tells us to "weep with those who weep" (Romans 12:15) because when we do, we reflect his heart. God's laughter is connected to his justice. He laughs at those who think they can avoid it. God can laugh at the devil because of his superior knowledge, power, and authority.

I was reminded of God's superior knowledge in an odd way when I watched the movie *Ocean's Eleven,* the story of a casino robbery. The robbery succeeded because the thieves knew the casino owner so well. They spent time watching his every move, how he reacted under pressure, what was important to him, and what his objectives were.

By the time the robbery was in progress, the thieves were able to maneuver the owner into being where they wanted him to be and seeing what they wanted him to see. The owner thought he had a foolproof security system, but it was thwarted by the thieves's superior knowledge.[1]

Likewise, God knows the devil's every move. Centuries before it happens, Isaiah prophesies the death of God's Son with startling detail (Isaiah 53). If the devil had realized God's plan, he wouldn't have arranged for Jesus's death. "But the rulers of this world have not understood it; if they had, they would not have crucified our glorious Lord" (1 Corinthians 2:8).

God doesn't initiate evil. But sometimes he withholds his presence, and the devil has an opportunity. The sun doesn't cause darkness, but rather at nightfall, when the sun appears to withdraw, we're in the dark. Similarly, sometimes God withdraws his light, and the devil takes advantage.

Meanwhile, God works behind the scenes, orchestrating events to bring about his outcomes. In Revelation, through imagery and allegory, God foretells the devil's ultimate defeat. Evil doesn't have free reign but operates only until God's purposes are accomplished. God can even use evil to bring about good outcomes, which is remarkable. "And we know that God causes everything to work together for the good of those who love God and are called according to his purpose for them" (Romans 8:28).

"Everything" includes those things that God allows, even if the source is evil. We can rest in the assurance that God would never allow anything evil to happen unless the outcome is good.

One Night in a Bad Hotel

Nevertheless, suffering is hard to understand. Many refuse to believe in a compassionate God because of the suffering in the world, and the devil does all he can to reinforce this view. The world's concept of Christianity is far too small. Christianity doesn't simply ask us to believe in a compassionate God. Rather, it asks us to believe in a whole spiritual realm that's far more real and enduring than the visible world. We look at the visible world, see that human beings are the highest life form, and incorrectly assume that life is all about us. But it's not.

Life is about God and his eternal kingdom.

We can make sense of suffering only if we take the long-term, eternal view and believe in a God who will ultimately bring justice. Mother Teresa had an amazing vision of her heavenly home. She worked among those who were dying from AIDS, tuberculosis, and other terminal diseases. She must have seen immense suffering. But she rather shockingly wrote, "In light of heaven, the worst suffering on earth, a life full of the most atrocious tortures on earth, will be seen to be no more serious than one night in an inconvenient hotel."[2]

One night in a bad hotel. Seriously?

God gives John an amazing vision of our future home (Revelation 21:2–4). Mother Teresa and John understood our human perspective is small.

When we look at the world, we don't see God's ultimate control. We see evil apparently winning. At such times, we need to trust in God's character and rely on his goodness, believing that one day everything will make sense. In the meantime, we remind ourselves of God's all-powerfulness, like the woman described in Proverbs. "She is clothed with strength and dignity, and she laughs without fear of the future" (Proverbs 31:25).

God calls us to be those who laugh without fear of the future. We can laugh if we have faith in God's eternal sovereignty. Our faith will keep us joyful when we have the assurance that this world is temporary and there's no need to fear the future since God is never caught by surprise.

We can live securely in the knowledge that God is never the initiator of evil and our lives are safe in his hands.

Job and Suffering

Job reveals some important truths about the devil. God toys with the devil and sets him up for a premeditated defeat, since it's God who brings up the subject of Job, deliberately provoking the devil. "Have you noticed my servant Job? He is the finest man in all the earth. He is blameless—a man of complete integrity. He fears God and stays away from evil" (Job 1:8).

The devil challenges God with the words, "Yes, but Job has good reason to fear God" (Job 1:9). He suggests that Job obeys God only because he blesses him with protection.

God withdraws his protection from Job, and he's inflicted with a series of disasters. Yet God is always in control. The devil ultimately is proven wrong. Job maintains his faith, even when he isn't blessed and doesn't understand why he's suffering.

When we read the story, we identify with Job and

wonder why God allows him to go through such misery. Job isn't aware of God's conversation with the devil, but we're given a glimpse into the heavenly realm, and we know Job isn't suffering as a result of his sin. God calls him "blameless," but Job's friends are oblivious to this.

Early in the book, we find that Job lives with a lot of fear and dread. He regularly makes offerings on behalf of his children, just in case they've sinned. "He would get up early in the morning and offer a burnt offering for each of them. For Job said to himself, 'Perhaps my children have sinned and have cursed God in their hearts.' This was Job's regular practice" (Job 1:5).

Job lives with a lot of 'what ifs' and 'just in case.' He tries to live a safe life and plans for every contingency. He's not trusting God to look after him.

After he's beset with troubles, he says, "What I always feared has happened to me. What I dreaded has come true" (Job 3:25).

Job is a fearful person.
It's not how God intends us to live.

After going through the trials, Job experiences God's presence, and he comes to a place of greater confidence in God. He experiences freedom from fear and a larger faith in God. He says, "I had only heard about you before, but now I have seen you with my own eyes" (Job 42:5).

Our response to trouble is often to wonder if God has forgotten us. The truth is the exact opposite. God uses our difficulties to draw us into a deeper relationship with him. In a rare piece of insight, Job's young friend, Elihu, says to him,

> He is wooing you from the jaws of distress
> to a spacious place free from restriction,
> to the comfort of your table
> laden with choice food.
> (Job 36:16 NIV)

At the end of his trials, Job knows he no longer has to live in fear, not because nothing distressing will ever happen to him again but because he knows God will sustain him.

God always has something more for us. Job is already "blameless," but God wants him, and us, free from fear. And sometimes, he will use trouble to get us there.

Standing

When we find ourselves facing a challenge or an unexpected turn of events, Paul calls us to stand firm. "Don't be intimidated in any way by your enemies. This will be a sign to them that they are going to be destroyed, but that you are going to be saved, even by God himself" (Philippians 1:28).

I often find parallels between sports and life. I watched the playoff hole between two top golfers in the Australian Masters Golf Championship a few years ago. Both players took two shots to land on the green. By then, a large crowd had gathered and followed the players up the fairway. The first player, the ultimate winner, was slightly farther away and had the first attempt at a birdie putt. He opted to play a safe shot that missed the hole by a few centimeters. He then tapped the ball in for an easy par.

The second player knew a successful putt would secure the championship. Two putts would mean playing another hole. You could feel the tension even in my lounge room. He missed. The crowd groaned. Nevertheless, he could still salvage the situation if he holed his next shot. However, his first attempt had overshot the hole by a couple of meters, and he was unable to sink his next putt. His disappointment was profound. In minutes, he went from a winning position to being the runner-up.

The winner, when interviewed, said he attempted to hit the ball into the hole with one putt but also played it safe because he thought his opponent might miss. What an amazing statement! Here are professional golfers, who practice putting for hours a day, and yet he believed his opponent would struggle to hole the ball with one putt. In reality, he was saying, "I thought he might succumb under the pressure."

If the opponent had followed the example of the winner, he could have waited for a better opportunity, but he went for the winning shot too soon and missed.

This incident resonated with me. In the early days of our pastoral ministry, I would often see an opportunity to start a ministry, create a new group, or revitalize an old one. In my enthusiasm and impatience, I pushed ahead with my idea too hard and too quickly. I found people pulled back and weren't supportive. I'd squandered the chance to do something significant. If I had stood firm on my idea and waited for an opportunity, without being daunted and without forcing my idea, there would've been a better outcome.

We don't fight for victory. We stand in God's victory.

We can mistakenly think that by rushing in and making something happen, we're doing God's work. We forget we can't defeat the enemy by our own efforts. We don't need to worry about hitting winning shots or trying to look good in the eyes of the world. If we stand firm in the belief that God will bring about his purposes in his time, without being manipulative or domineering, we bring about the enemy's defeat.

A Stealer of Our Confidence

We give the devil far too much credit and even ascribe attributes to him that belong solely to God. Only God is all-knowing, all-powerful, and always present. The devil may have an army of demons, but he's not everywhere at once. He may have some power, but he's not all-powerful. He needs to ask God's permission (Luke 22:31). And, as we've seen, he's not all-knowing.

Biblical authors describe the devil as a thief (John 10:10), as a liar (John 8:44), and as capable of disguising himself as an angel of light (2 Corinthians 11:14). The devil aims to steal our confidence in God's goodness, love, and sovereignty. To achieve his purposes he uses his cunning and deceptive ways.

C. S. Lewis paints a vivid picture of the devil's deception in his book *The Silver Chair*, part of the Narnia series. The witch in the story traps the children underground. She tells them it was all a dream and there was never a place called Narnia or a lion called Aslan, who represents Jesus.

The children are on the verge of falling for the witch's lies when one of the non-human characters deliberately puts his foot in the fire. The pain wakes him up to the reality of what's going on. The witch was only bluffing.[3]

Lewis has depicted the illusory nature of evil. He demonstrates how the devil uses intimidation to cause us to lose our confidence. His allegory teaches us that the devil tricks us into focusing on what can be seen and makes the eternal seem like a dream. He lulls us into thinking what we can see is all there is instead of following Paul's instruction to fix our eyes on what cannot be seen (2 Corinthians 4:18).

The story also illustrates that often it's pain that wakes us up to the devil's lies.

Years ago, after Ross had been through chemotherapy, God drew my attention to these words:

> You captured us in your net
> and laid the burden of slavery on our backs.
> Then you put a leader over us.
> We went through fire and flood,
> but you brought us to a place of great abundance.
> (Psalm 66:11–12)

Ross's illness certainly felt like going through "fire and flood," but now, with the benefit of hindsight, I can see that God freed me from a life of trying to earn his approval. It wasn't until I reached the place where I no longer had the energy to do things to please God that I realized I didn't need to. God brought me to a place of security, knowing I already had his approval. A place where I could renounce the devil's lies. I'd certainly heard God's acceptance preached before Ross became unwell. Yet, I doubt I would have come to this personal understanding without going through a painful experience.

Only Pretending

The Israelites go through an extended painful experience which culminates in exile to Babylon. Jeremiah brings prophetic messages during this time. He begins his ministry in the thirteenth year of King Josiah's reign (Jeremiah 1:1–2). Josiah is a good king who reigns for thirty-one years and institutes some major reforms (2 Kings 22:1–2). He destroys many idols and heathen altars. He repairs the temple and reinstates the Passover (23:1–25). However, after Josiah's death, during the reigns of Josiah's sons, the people of Judah are exiled because of their sinful ways (2 Kings 24).

Josiah's reforms correct Judah's outward behavior but don't touch their hearts. "But despite all this, her faithless sister Judah has never sincerely returned to me. She has only pretended to be sorry" (Jeremiah 3:10).

The people of Judah follow King Josiah's decrees and think that will be enough to appease God. But God doesn't ask for an outward adherence to a set of rules. He desires a heartfelt relationship that transforms our attitudes and motives.

In Babylon, the exiles are a long way from the temple, the altar, and their sacrificial practices. They're without their outward forms of religion. If they want to worship and honor God in Babylon, it will have to be from their hearts. Being in exile is God's "severe mercy."[4] He takes away the outward trappings of their religion in the hope they would come to an inward faith.

Likewise, we may wonder why God allows a ministry or some other Christian activity to stop, even though it appears to be worthwhile. Sometimes, God has to strip away the external activity to reveal the lies the devil has sown and allow people to come to a place of greater freedom.

A Fly on the Wall

Since the devil doesn't know what we're thinking, a spoken confession is powerful against his attacks. "If you openly declare that Jesus is Lord and believe in your heart that God raised him from the dead, you will be saved" (Romans 10:9). When we declare with our voice that Jesus is Lord, we make a declaration of our faith that the powers of darkness wouldn't know unless we said it out loud.

The devil may suggest an idea to us or drop a thought into our thinking, but he doesn't know what we do with these thoughts unless he sees us acting on them. While he doesn't know what we're thinking, he does watch us.

The devil is the proverbial "fly on the wall."

Our actions are evidence of our beliefs. Do our words line up with our actions? We can easily say all the right Christian things, especially if we spend time in Christian circles. We can easily believe someone who is articulate with Christian terminology and sounds sincere. The true test of spirituality isn't how well we speak or how much we know but rather how we behave. If a person's behavior doesn't consistently line up with their words, then this is a more accurate indicator of their beliefs. If we say we love God but don't live in a way that pleases him, do we really love God? If we say we believe in the value of reading the Bible and prayer but never do either, then our actions reveal our true beliefs.

Nothing to Lose

When John writes to the churches in Revelation, he tells them there are three ways to stand in God's victory and overcome the devil.

> And they have defeated him by the
> blood of the Lamb
> and by their testimony.
> And they did not love their lives so much
> that they were afraid to die.
> (Revelation 12:11)

Often, we concentrate on the first two. We remember Jesus's sacrificial death, which gives us victory over sin and guilt, and our testimony reminds us of the way God has previously worked in our lives. The third way is not to love our lives so much that we're afraid to die. We often associate this with martyrs, but it also contains an important truth for us.

We become an easy target for the devil when we cling too tightly to the things of the world. We easily forget this world isn't our permanent address. We tend to hold on to those things that give us comfort and security, like our homes, our jobs, our family, our friends, our community, our health, our possessions, or our ministry at church. If we want to overcome the devil, we hold these things loosely. We commit the important things in our lives to God so that the devil cannot attack us with the fear of loss, grief, and death. When we aren't afraid of losing things that are precious to us, the devil suffers a defeat.

The devil cannot attack us with the fear of losing things if we have nothing to lose.

Spiritually, it's not easy to get to this place. Yet our comfort and security come from knowing we can't lose our most precious possession, our relationship with God, which will continue long after the things of this world have faded away.

As God's children, we've read the last page and know that, despite some skirmishes along the way, we win. We can laugh without fear of the future because we know that the devil's plans are limited, brief, and deceptive. God's laughter points to a future when evil is no longer present and laughter becomes about enjoying his presence.

"Then the angel showed me a river with the water of life, clear as crystal, flowing from the throne of God and of the Lamb" (Revelation 22:1). God's river of living water flowing from his throne creates beautiful images of a babbling brook laughing with the joy of being in his presence.

Let's Pray

Thank you, Lord, that you want me free from fear so, like the woman in Proverbs 31, I can laugh at the future. You are Ruler of all things. The devil is limited. I surrender to you knowing my life is safe in your hands.

Thank you, Lord, that you alone know what I'm thinking, and I pray you will purify my thoughts and my attitudes. May my actions be in line with my stated beliefs.

In times of suffering, remind me that you are working to bring me to a place of greater blessing.

Help me to stand firm on your promises and not be frightened by those who oppose me, knowing that I don't have to fight for victory. Rather I stand in your victory.

In Jesus's name.
Amen.

Conclusion

The image of a good God who blesses his people isn't as welcome as you'd expect. I've met people in churches who picture God as a legalist, a taskmaster, or a spoilsport.

There's a certain logic and comfort in holding on to wrong concepts of God. If we like being a workaholic, we can excuse our behavior if we believe God is a hard taskmaster. Likewise, if we're inclined to push the boundaries of God's standards for our behavior, we can imagine God as an indulgent grandfather. If we can't cope with God being mysterious, we can invent our own reasons for God's ways rather than embracing the unknown. Our understanding of God becomes distorted when we do this, but it's easier to justify avoiding, ignoring, or dismissing his claims.

What good reason could there possibly be for not committing to a loving God who wants to bless us? Yet here are three reasons why we might hesitate to trust God with our lives.

1st Reason—Spiritual Maturity

A good God who wants our happiness also wants us to grow spiritually so we can experience more of his love, joy, and peace. He wants us to give up our ways of finding comfort and security and trust his ways.

God wants us to surrender our independent self, that part of us that likes to do things our way. That part of us that is comfortable with the way things are, that doesn't want to be challenged or taken outside our comfort zone. A good God who wants our happiness also wants us to part with something—our lesser self.

God knows we'll be happiest when we are the best versions of ourselves. The anxious and fearful versions cannot sustain God's joy, so God will do whatever it takes to make us suitable receptacles. How willing are we to trust God's methods?

"Because of the joy awaiting him, he [Jesus] endured the cross, disregarding its shame" (Hebrews 12:2).

Not only did joy await Jesus, but joy also awaits us.

Our pathway also involves dying to our ambitions and agendas. Plus dying to the pretend versions of ourselves that project an image that's acceptable to others. It's difficult to trust God when he prunes and refines us to make us better versions of ourselves.

Growing spiritually mature is also difficult because it takes so long. During Ross's recovery from cancer, I wasn't coping well, so I asked God to "fix" me. God drew my attention to this verse.

> In that day their burden will be lifted
> from your shoulders,
> their yoke from your neck;
> the yoke will be broken
> because you have grown so fat.
> (Isaiah 10:27 NIV)

In Isaiah's time, farmers would place a wooden frame, a yoke, across the shoulders of two animals to keep them in tandem as they worked. Thomas Constable explains, "God's blessing on his people would be responsible for the breaking of the yoke of bondage on them."[1]

God used this illustration to explain to me how he would answer my prayers, not by an instant miracle but by steady spiritual growth. I must admit I was disappointed. I wanted a solution yesterday, but any time today would be good! However, God knows quick change is generally not lasting.

Spiritual growth can be so slow it's hard to detect. Yet over time, we will see a difference. The "yoke" in our life might be a bad habit, a phobia, or some other persistent problem. Like me, you might pray for God to remove it, but instead, God might want to break it through the gradual process of spiritual growth. Over time, we'll notice our mindset changing, our motives purifying, and our responses being less negative. We will notice that things that challenged us in the past no longer do because we've grown spiritually "fat."

Spiritual growth is little by little, like the work of the ant. The ant achieves a lot by doing a little often. As we consistently and regularly learn, little by little, change happens.

2nd Reason—Representing Him Well

What about when life is going well? Do we trust God in those times? Do we continue to seek his blessings when we're doing well without them?

One of God's purposes in blessing his people is to show

others what a blessing it is to belong to God. "Everyone will realize that they are a people the Lord has blessed" (Isaiah 61:9).

If we don't continually seek God's blessing, we deprive our world of knowing how good it is to live God's ways. God seeks to build our trust in him so he can bless us and bless others through us. He wants us to continually seek his blessings, even at those times when we think we don't particularly need them.

People watch us to see if being a Christian makes any difference in our lives. We may feel this isn't something we signed up for when we became Christians. Peter writes, "And if someone asks about your hope as a believer, always be ready to explain it" (1 Peter 3:15).

For a long time, I didn't tell anyone I was a Christian, and I seriously hoped no one would ask. I didn't like the idea of being watched by those around me to see if being a Christian makes a difference. Moses knew there ought to be something different about God's people. In the wilderness, Moses says to God, "For your presence among us sets your people and me apart from all other people on the earth" (Exodus 33:16).

Indeed, the presence of God sets us apart. Moses knew it wasn't outward observances of rituals, being law-abiding citizens, or even helping people in need. The thing that sets us apart is the presence of God radiating from our lives. It ought to be apparent to others that we have a supernatural source of power. A power that causes us to be more loving, joyful, peaceful, patient, caring, virtuous, faithful, gentle, and self-controlled (Galatians 5:22–23).

Is this fruit evident in our lives? Or are our lives indistinguishable from those people who are reliable, responsible, and respectable members of our community?

Moses knew the presence of God made the difference. Jesus told his disciples they would be known for their love. "Your love for one another will prove to the world that you are my disciples" (John 13:35).

We would prefer more concrete evidence for being a Christian.

The early church sometimes became distracted by rules and regulations, like dietary laws, because these could provide obvious evidence of whether someone was a true believer or not (Colossians 2:16). In the same way, we can become distracted by external activities and focus more on what Christians do or don't do, what social venues they visit or avoid, or how often they attend church-related activities. But this isn't the evidence Jesus looks for in his disciples.

We may be tempted to gauge spiritual maturity by someone's abilities or gifts. Some can rattle off Bible verses from memory with great ease, which is a wonderful ability, but it doesn't necessarily make them more mature. God may have just given them a great memory.

Sometimes, we're impressed with how much Bible knowledge someone has or how they pray. Perhaps they pray with great fervor or with great mastery of the English language, which is a pleasure to listen to, but again, this isn't a test of maturity. The acid test is how loving we are. Paul tells Timothy, "The purpose of my instruction is that all believers would be filled with love that comes from a pure heart, a clear conscience, and genuine faith" (1 Timothy 1:5).

The aim of any spiritual discipline isn't that we get an A+ in theology. The aim is to become more loving, which is a far bigger challenge.

3rd Reason—Correct Expectations

I've heard nonbelievers say they don't need God as their life is going fine without him. This disturbs me since it sounds like God exists for my convenience, to fix my problems, and to keep me happy. This view fails to acknowledge his sovereignty and his Lordship. This world isn't all there is, and life isn't about me.

God doesn't exist for our convenience. Rather we live for his cause.

The Westminster Catechism, written in the seventeenth century, states that our chief end "is to glorify God, and to enjoy him forever."[2] In the Christian circles I move in, this doesn't seem widely known or experienced.

The statement summarizes the Christian life so well. If we want to glorify God, we will live in a way that pleases him. This isn't a life of religious burden but rather an enjoyable one in which we delight in God and his blessings. It implies we're completely secure, serene, and satisfied in our relationship with God.

Will we glorify God and enjoy him forever?

On the Flying Trapeze

I've mentioned that my husband and I have lived in many

different towns. We initially relocated when Ross received promotions from the bank. Those moves were relatively easy because the bank organized a moving company, paid us traveling time, and continued all our entitlements. However, moving to take up different pastoral positions was more problematic. Every time we accepted a new position, even when it was with the same denomination in the same state, it was like starting a brand-new job with a new employer. All our leave entitlements were paid out. We then used these funds for our traveling and resettling expenses.

There were times when we believed God led us to finish at one church before we were entirely sure where we were going next. I felt like we were on a flying trapeze. We had to let go of one swing and hope the other swing arrived before we hit financial ground zero. God was faithful, and our trust in him grew. The swing always arrived in time, though often we were hanging in mid-air for longer than I liked.

What about you? Will you trust God on the flying trapezes of life?

God puts us through experiences that build our trust in him. These experiences are unique to each of us. The more we understand that God's intentions are good, the more we trust God, and the more we're able to receive his many blessings. Paul writes, "Since he did not spare even his own Son but gave him up for us all, won't he also give us everything else?" (Romans 8:32).

When we consider the cross and know God wouldn't even spare his Son, we know he will provide everything else we need. God is for us. And he has proven it by giving up his Son. Whatever the situation, God is for us. Certainly, he may convict, confront, or challenge us, but his motives are good. He has our best interests at heart and wants to bless us with good things. But how do we respond?

This is the challenge I've sought to address throughout this book. Will we trust God to bless us? Will we continually seek his blessings, even if we think we don't need or want them?

Will we trust him when he calls us to life on the flying trapeze?

10 Blessings of God
You Won't Want To Miss

With Study Guide

SUSAN BARNES

Contents

Introduction to the Study Guide   179

God Shares His Happiness   181

God Surprises   184

God Frees   187

God Identifies with Us   190

God Loves   193

God Gives Hope   196

God Has a Plan   199

God Blesses   202

God Gives Peace   205

God Overcomes   208

Conclusion   211

Acknowledgements   213

Endnotes   215

Next book in 2026   219

Introduction to the Study Guide

Gathering with God's people to discuss his Word and its practical implications is an enriching experience. The benefits of studying biblical concepts in small groups go beyond having a better intellectual understanding of the Bible. Equally important is the sense of mutual support and community. Paul experienced this in Thessalonica. "We loved you so much that we shared with you not only God's Good News but our own lives, too" (1 Thessalonians 2:8).

I hope your group also shares your lives with one another as you consider the question asked in the book's introduction. Do God's blessings make a practical difference in your daily life?

The first two questions for each chapter, based on the titles of the chapter breaks and the statements in the callout boxes, aim to encourage the group to discuss the general topic and share personal experiences. The questions that follow don't need to be answered in order or strictly adhered to as long as the discussion is relevant and beneficial to participants. The summary from each chapter of the book has been included in the study guide as an overview of the topic.

Group members can download a PDF of the study guide (www.susanbarneswriter.com). An email address is required to download. I hope using this study guide helps you experience God's many blessings.

1

God Shares His Happiness

Summary

Jesus is happy and full of joy. This teaches us an important truth—if Jesus is happy, we can be too. He calls us to share his happiness. But will we?

As we consider biblical passages that speak about joy, we learn that God wants us to experience his joy more often than we do. He wants us to share his happiness. Worshiping God brings us joy because it takes our attention off ourselves and places it on God and his kingdom. This helps us to take the long-term perspective since we realize this world isn't all there is and our time here is very brief.

Beware of joy stealers, like worry, frustration, discontent, intimidation, time constraints, trying to control our circumstances, and the fear of dying before we reach our goals. These things don't keep God from being happy, and they don't have to keep us from happiness either. We can learn how to overcome joy stealers.

We reconcile a happy God and his anger by understanding he is angry over injustice. Ultimately, we will see the destruction of evil. A new world is coming where there will be no more pain. In the meantime, we can be happy.

Discussion Questions

1. Which section of the chapter was the most meaningful for you?
   - Jesus, Happy and Joyful
   - God's Self-Portrait
   - Becoming Happy
   - Joy Stealers
   - God's Anger
   - The God Perspective
   - Ways to Increase Happiness

2. Which of these statements surprised, comforted or challenged you?
   - God is happy, and he invites us to share his happiness.
   - God passionately desires a relationship with people.
   - We worship so we can stop being the center of our attention.
   - Injustice angers God.
   - God knew creating people with free will was deeply problematic.
   - A new world is coming where there will be no more pain.

3. Identify the joy stealers in your life. How will you overcome these?

4. What can you do to remind yourself of God's larger perspective?

5. How can you engage more during times of worship so your attention is off yourself and on God?

6. Have you considered that the anger of God is a natural outworking of his love? How does this encourage your trust in God?

7. What steps will you take to increase your level of happiness?

8. In what ways has this chapter changed or confirmed your thinking?

2

God Surprises

Summary

God surprises us with his generous care, his foresight, and his intimate involvement in our lives, but are we paying attention or taking these things for granted?

King David wants to build a temple for God. Instead God surprises him by promising to build his family into a lasting dynasty. David is so surprised he wonders if it's normal.

During Jesus's time on earth, he was unpredictable. His miracles surprise us by their abundant provision or because he performed them for those we might consider undeserving. Sometimes, even Jesus was surprised, he didn't always know what God was going to do.

What prevents us from being surprised?

We stop being surprised when we forget God's blessings and focus on our difficulties. If God doesn't answer our prayers the way we expect, it can tempt us to harbor dissatisfaction. Dissatisfaction can lead to complaining when we fail to pay attention to the many spiritual and physical blessings God has given to us. Paul instructs us to learn to be content.

Jesus's death on the cross is very familiar to us. Do we

allow the magnitude of God's sacrifice to overwhelm us with gratitude and surprise that God would be so good to us?

Discussion Questions

1. Which section of the chapter was the most meaningful for you?
   - God's Surprise for David
   - Unpredictability
   - More Surprises
   - Paying Attention
   - Taken for Granted
   - Surprise Stealers
   - Disappointment

2. Which of these statements surprised, comforted or challenged you?
   - God wants to surprise us.
   - The life of faith is an adventure: Are we willing to be surprised?
   - I'm tempted to reduce my relationship with God to a formula.
   - God doesn't just want to meet our needs. He wants to provide more than enough.
   - God hates it when I gripe.
   - Finding satisfaction in God takes faith, and this glorifies him.

3. What's the most surprising thing God has done in your life? Or the most surprising answer to prayer that you have had?

4. Has your connection with God ever felt more like a formula than a relationship? What can you do to change this?

5. Which stories in the Gospels surprise you the most? Do you find Jesus surprising?

6. Are you satisfied with God? Or are there aspects of your appearance, your personality, or your circumstances that you wish God would change?

7. When have you had reason to think, "I can't believe God would be so good to me?

8. In what ways has this chapter changed or confirmed your thinking?

allow the magnitude of God's sacrifice to overwhelm us with gratitude and surprise that God would be so good to us?

Discussion Questions

1. Which section of the chapter was the most meaningful for you?
   - God's Surprise for David
   - Unpredictability
   - More Surprises
   - Paying Attention
   - Taken for Granted
   - Surprise Stealers
   - Disappointment

2. Which of these statements surprised, comforted or challenged you?
   - God wants to surprise us.
   - The life of faith is an adventure: Are we willing to be surprised?
   - I'm tempted to reduce my relationship with God to a formula.
   - God doesn't just want to meet our needs. He wants to provide more than enough.
   - God hates it when I gripe.
   - Finding satisfaction in God takes faith, and this glorifies him.

3. What's the most surprising thing God has done in your life? Or the most surprising answer to prayer that you have had?

4. Has your connection with God ever felt more like a formula than a relationship? What can you do to change this?

5. Which stories in the Gospels surprise you the most? Do you find Jesus surprising?

6. Are you satisfied with God? Or are there aspects of your appearance, your personality, or your circumstances that you wish God would change?

7. When have you had reason to think, "I can't believe God would be so good to me?

8. In what ways has this chapter changed or confirmed your thinking?

3

God Frees

Summary

We can enjoy up-to-the-minute forgiveness and freedom from keeping track of our sins. As we walk in God's ways, his blood continually cleanses us from all wrongdoing. God deals so completely with our sins that he calls us "saints."

Jesus changes us not by our efforts but by his Spirit. He gives us righteousness as a gift, and we don't lose the gift if we sin. God's grace will motivate and enable us to avoid those things that displease him.

Still, freedom stealers threaten. We fall back into the habit of trying harder rather than trusting more when our behavior disappoints us. Rule-keeping also appeals, as it clearly defines wrong behavior. Yet God desires our freedom from rules and gives us principles instead. God wants us to rely on him in our decision making, rather than mindlessly following rules. This may differ from person to person, as we have different giftings and different levels of spiritual maturity. God gives us his peace and his Spirit to lead and guide us, and that's enough.

God's grace is freely available and abundant, enabling us to live like saints, but will we receive this grace?

Discussion Questions

1. Which section of the chapter was the most meaningful for you?
   - Up-to-the-Minute Forgiveness
   - Freedom Stealers
   - Another Freedom Stealer
   - The Point of the Law
   - Missing the Point
   - Man-Made Rules
   - Yes-No Answers
   - Seems Good
   - Out of Reverence

2. Which of these statements surprised, comforted or challenged you?
   - He lavishes us with his grace, so we can live guilt-free.
   - We are saints.
   - Jesus changes us by his Spirit, not by us trying to give ourselves an upgrade.
   - Creating rules for good behavior doesn't promote God's cause.
   - God's Spirit and his peace guide us, and it's enough.
   - God is more interested in *why* we do something than in *what* we do.

3. When are you tempted to fall for the freedom stealers of trying harder and rule-keeping?

4. What is the purpose of the Old Testament law?

5. What do you think would happen if we advertised Christianity as a lifestyle with no rules?

6. On what occasions are you likely to become so absorbed in what you're doing that you forget about God, even when the captivating thing is godly?

7. Can you give an example of a time when you made a decision because "it seemed good to the Holy Spirit"?

8. In what ways has this chapter changed or confirmed your thinking?

4.

God Identifies with Us

Summary

Jesus appearing in a body is an amazing mystery. That God would become a man should flabbergast us every time we think of it. His coming to earth displays God's desire to identify with us and means Jesus truly understands our particular needs in every situation. For thirty years he lives an ordinary life, so much so that no one realizes he is the Messiah, not even his own family. God has to reveal this knowledge to John the Baptist by giving him a specific sign.

When we study the historical context and culture of the Gospels, we notice that Jesus's stories are surprisingly pointed. Sometimes it feels like he knows us too well. Yet he uses his knowledge of us not to shame us but to help us. Since Jesus became fully human, he understands our weaknesses, so we can boldly approach God's throne. He knows how we feel when we go through difficulties and how to support us.

The devil tempts us to draw back from God in fear or shame. He wants us to doubt our standing with God and lose the assurance of his presence. Yet God has done everything to encourage us to come to him.

Will we connect with this God who knows us so well?

Discussion Questions

1. Which section of the chapter was the most meaningful for you?
   - Jesus's Earthly Life
   - Empathy
   - Our Identity Can't Be Stolen
   - Up Close and Personal
   - Fully Known
   - Jesus in Pain

2. Which of these statements surprised, comforted or challenged you?
   - God identifies with us by becoming a fully human, ordinary person.
   - God tears heaven in two to be with us.
   - It's important to see ourselves in the same way God sees us.
   - Jesus has a habit of taking conversations to places we don't want to go.
   - Jesus addresses his message to their exact situation.
   - However, some aren't ready to come to receive mercy and grace.

3. God becoming one of us is astounding. What impact does this have on your Christian walk?

4. Is it easy or difficult to imagine Jesus as an ordinary child, growing up in an ordinary family?

5. How do you feel about Jesus telling such insightful stories?

6. What steals your assurance of God's presence and what enhances it?

7. How do you feel about God being up close and personal?

8. In what ways has this chapter changed or confirmed your thinking?

5.

God Loves

Summary

Many times, we've been told that God loves us, but our fears tell us we aren't fully convinced. Will we open our hearts to this great love?

Hard things happen in our lives, but it doesn't mean God doesn't care about us. God uses our difficulties for our spiritual growth. He's like a good parent who protects his children from unnecessary harm, though not always from pain, and sometimes makes choices we don't understand.

We may read about God's judgments in the Old Testament and wonder about God's love. We underestimate how sin offends God's holiness. Nevertheless, we see evidence of God's love and grace in the lives of many people in the Old Testament.

God longs for a close, intimate relationship with his people. We may find obstacles and challenges that threaten to steal our trust in God's love, but we can remember the sacrifices God made for us, which reveal the depths of his love. He sent Jesus in response to the devastating effects of sin and evil. When we reflect on the cross, we know God loves us.

Discussion Questions

1. Which section of the chapter was the most meaningful for you?
   - Free from Fear
   - God the Good Parent
   - Intimacy
   - Without the Right Motivation
   - Obstacles that Steal
   - For a Little While
   - Loving God for Himself
   - Love in Action

2. Which of these statements surprised, comforted or challenged you?
   - God loves us—completely, unconditionally, extravagantly, endlessly.
   - God is a good parent who protects us from unnecessary harm, but not always from pain.
   - God freely employs the intimate symbols of marriage and sex to demonstrate how he feels about his people.
   - God is holy and just. Every sin is worthy of the death penalty.
   - Through the cross, we learn how valuable we are to him and how much he loves us.
   - Furthermore, we make sacrifices for those we love.

3. What are you afraid of? Would you still be afraid if you were completely convinced God loved you?

4. Why do you think God uses the imagery of marriage to describe our relationship with him?

5. Does the harshness of some of the Old Testament stories bother you? How do you reconcile this with Jesus's compassion?

6. How does knowing our separation from God is "for a little while" bring us comfort in difficult times?

7. How do you know if someone loves you?

8. In what ways has this chapter changed or confirmed your thinking?

6

God Gives Hope

Summary

Do we hope for better circumstances? Or do we hope in God?

Biblical hope is an anchor for our souls. It looks back to the cross, where God interrupted history to restore our relationship with him, and looks forward to the time when God will again enter history to bring justice and restoration. Hope gives Paul the confidence to declare his troubles to be small and temporary because of future glory.

However, it's difficult to develop hope if we rely on our achievements, our possessions, or our wisdom. Worldly things are an unreliable source of hope as they can be taken away from us through a downturn in the economy, ill health, untimely accidents or other events we have no control over. Furthermore, our hope can be stolen from us if we look at only our physical circumstances or trust only what our senses tell us. Hagar's, Moses's, and Jonah's experiences all encourage our hope.

Jesus showed enormous hope by picking twelve unlikely men to be his disciples and agents of a spiritual revolution. This gives us hope for our churches and Christian leadership.

Peter encourages us to remember we have been born again into a living hope through Jesus's resurrection.

Circumstances are never so bad that it's too late to hope in God.

Discussion Questions

1. Which section of the chapter was the most meaningful for you?
   - Hope—Not Just for Now
   - Future Glory
   - Obstacles to Hope
   - Hope Beyond Our Senses
   - Hope in Hopelessness
   - Stolen Hope
   - Never Too Late
   - Rewarded
   - Certain Hope

2. Which of these statements surprised, comforted or challenged you?
   - God gives hope—a hope that is sure, steadfast, unwavering, and unshakable despite any upheavals in the world or our lives.
   - Future glory outweighs present inconveniences.
   - Cultivating hope is difficult when we rely on our own resources.
   - Yet Jesus's followers change the world.
   - God sees our distress and hears our cries.
   - It's never too late to hope in God.

3. How would you explain the difference between

worldly hope and biblical hope?

4. When you're facing difficulties, what impact does knowing God has good purposes in mind have on you?

5. Consider the personality flaws of the twelve disciples. How does this inspire you to follow Jesus?

6. When have you used God's promise of rewards to motivate and encourage yourself?

7. What can you do to cultivate biblical hope?

8. In what ways has this chapter changed or confirmed your thinking?

7

God Has a Plan

Summary

God's eternal plan is to bless all nations. God intends for his Body, the church, to show the world how good it is to live according to his ways.

God's plan for us isn't one long to-do list since there's only one thing on God's list: Become like Jesus. This is both a blessing and a challenge. It's a blessing because we can't miss God's plan or have it stolen from us. It's a challenge because he may take us out of our comfort zone to achieve this goal.

We may feel we've missed God's tasks for our lives but a lack of positive outcomes doesn't necessarily mean we're off track. Amos, Paul, Isaiah, and others suffered opposition and an apparent lack of success in the places God sent them. Time gives us a different perspective on success and teaches us to leave the results to God.

We discover the places God wants us to serve by noticing the circumstances and Scriptures that God brings to our attention. This will be different for everyone, depending on the unique way he has gifted us.

At the end of time, God will be able to explain everything. This gives us confidence and encouragement to persist in following God's guidance.

Discussion Questions

1. Which section of the chapter was the most meaningful for you?
   - Special Treasure
   - The Church
   - One Task
   - God's Projects
   - Becoming Christlike
   - Flexible Plans
   - Detours
   - Finding the Race God Has for Us
   - Do God's Plans Fail?
   - God Can Explain

2. Which of these statements surprised, comforted or challenged you?
   - God has a plan. It's a vast, all-encompassing, amazing, eternal plan.
   - God plans to make us more and more like Christ.
   - We're God's masterpiece, his handiwork, his project.
   - God's enabling is enough for any task.
   - We run our race and not someone else's.
   - One day, God will explain everything, or maybe it will be obvious.

3. Describe your understanding of God's plans.

4. Have you ever felt you've missed God because circumstances haven't worked out the way you believed God intended?

5. Opposition didn't deter Paul from preaching in Macedonia or Isaiah from preaching in Israel. The opposition we face today is often more subtle—the withdrawal of friendship, the withholding of information, the lack of an invitation. What is your experience of opposition?

6. How do you keep going when you experience a lack of success in what you believe God asks you to do?

7. Do you have confidence that at the end of time, God will explain everything? What are the Bible verses or answers to prayer that encourage you to persist in trusting God's plans (e.g., Ephesians 2:10)?

8. In what ways has this chapter changed or confirmed your thinking?

8

God Blesses

Summary

God has blessed us by providing salvation. Yet he also seeks to bless us in our daily lives and waits for us to open our hearts so we can be good receivers. However, some struggle to believe God desires to bless them, especially if their circumstances currently show no evidence of this.

Furthermore, sometimes friends or family may try to bless us, but it may be difficult to recognize or accept their kindness if it doesn't meet our expectations. Many find it easier to give than receive, but if we aren't good receivers, we deprive others of the blessing of giving.

Jesus gives us the Beatitudes to teach us how to develop the attitudes that would make us better recipients of God's blessings. He tells us to be prepared to ask and cultivate a childlike attitude. As we persist in our Christian walk, we'll discover blessings only God could provide.

When we discover people who aren't living a godly life yet experience God's blessing, we may feel confused or offended, but these incidents remind us of God's graciousness.

Are we open to receiving all that God has for us? Ultimately, as we grow in our relationship with God, we trust him to bless us with whatever he determines is best for us.

Discussion Questions

1. Which section of the chapter was the most meaningful for you?
   - Let God love you
   - Receiving
   - God Blesses
   - Honors
   - Ask
   - Becoming Good Receivers
   - Blessing Disobedience?
   - A Miracle

2. Which of these statements surprised, comforted or challenged you?
   - God blesses us—first with salvation, but also in many other ways, unexpectedly, undeservedly, lavishly.
   - Some won't receive from God. How sad.
   - Be on the lookout for blessings only God can provide.
   - Our prayers do impact circumstances.
   - Although, we can't assume God's blessing indicates his approval.
   - He blesses us so we can be a blessing to others.

3. Have you ever wrestled with an apparent lack of evidence of God's blessings?

4. In what circumstances have you struggled to understand why God seems to bless some people more than others?

5. Have there been times when you found it difficult to ask God for your own needs?

6. Which of the Beatitudes do you find the hardest to apply? Or the easiest?

7. Is your life a miracle? What would your life look like if God wasn't part of it?

8. In what ways has this chapter changed or confirmed your thinking?

9

God Gives Peace

Summary

God wants us to rest in him so he can give us peace, not because we've earned it but because it's a gift. God isn't an unpleasable slave driver or taskmaster. He gave the Israelites specific days and festivals so they would rest. However, it means being prepared to trust God and receive peace even when we're facing difficult situations, like Gideon, who finds God's peace before the conflict is resolved.

Fear and worry will steal our peace. We control these emotions by taking responsibility for what we think about. As we change our thinking and focus on those things that build up our faith in God, we receive his peace.

As well as Jesus promising us peace, both Jesus and Paul tell his followers to expect trouble. In Jesus, we have peace, but not necessarily in our circumstances. We trust God, not because he removes our problems but because he is good and his sovereignty is never under threat. We trust his character knowing a good God will supply us with grace as we need it so we can cope with any crisis.

Discussion Questions

1. Which section of the chapter was the most meaningful for you?
   - Rest for My Soul
   - A Good King
   - Shalom
   - Stay Calm
   - God's Goodness
   - Peace Stealers
   - Being in Charge of Our Hearts
   - Tearing Your Clothes
   - Peace in Trouble

2. Which of these statements surprised, comforted or challenged you?
   - God wants me to rest in him, so he can give me peace.
   - We make a difference because God is with us.
   - God's sovereignty is never under threat, so we can experience peace.
   - Worrying achieves nothing, but it does rob us of peace.
   - Note well: God's help is supplied as needed, not in advance.
   - Trouble is part of our calling.

3. Describe a situation when you successfully or unsuccessfully remained peaceful in a difficult situation.

4. Can you relate an occasion when your responses to God were similar to Gideon's? Why Lord?

How Lord (Judges 6:13–15)?

5. Previous generations have had different understandings of resting on the Sabbath or Sunday (Hebrews 4). What are your thoughts?

6. What changes can you make that would renew your thinking so it's more in line with God's truth?

7. What can you do to more deeply enter God's rest and receive his peace?

8. In what ways has this chapter changed or confirmed your thinking?

10

God Overcomes

Summary

God calls us to be those who laugh without fear of the future and who stand firm in his victory, knowing he is ruler over all things and evil will ultimately be defeated. The devil is on a limited time frame and can do nothing without God's permission. Therefore God merely laughs at the feeble attempts of the wicked to thwart his purposes.

We give the devil far too much credit and even ascribe attributes to him that belong solely to God. The devil is a thief and liar. He attempts to steal our confidence in God's sovereignty.

Only God knows what we're thinking. However, the devil is the proverbial "fly on the wall" and watches to see if our actions match our words.

God has equipped us to overcome the devil. We don't fight for victory, rather we stand in the victory God has already won. Laughter is a foretaste of the future, when we will enjoy his presence and evil will no longer be present.

I started this book by looking at Jesus being happy and I'm finishing with God's laughter. In between, I hope you've seen that God longs for us to open our hearts to him so he can bless us and we can enjoy his favor.

Discussion Questions

1. Which section of the chapter was the most meaningful for you?
   - The Devil's Strategy
   - One Night in a Bad Hotel
   - Job and Suffering
   - Standing
   - A Stealer of Our Confidence
   - Only Pretending
   - A Fly on the Wall
   - Nothing to Lose

2. Which of these statements surprised, comforted or challenged you?
   - God overcomes evil gloriously, victoriously, and jubilantly.
   - Life is about God and his eternal kingdom.
   - Job is a fearful person. It's not how God intends us to live.
   - We don't fight for victory. We stand in God's victory.
   - The devil is the proverbial "fly on the wall."
   - The devil cannot attack us with the fear of losing things if we have nothing to lose.

3. Describe a difficult time in your life when you went through "fire" and "water" and came to a place of greater freedom.

4. Do you relate to the devil being the proverbial "fly

on the wall"? Will it make a difference to your lifestyle choices?

5. "In light of heaven, the worst suffering on earth, a life full of the most atrocious tortures on earth, will be seen to be no more serious than one night in an inconvenient hotel." Does this quote make you cringe at its impossibility? Or does Mother Teresa's view of suffering change your perspective?

6. Can you think of a time when you stood your ground and waited for God to come through for you? Or a time when you didn't?

7. In what ways does God laughing and Jesus being happy encourage your faith?

8. In what ways has this chapter changed or confirmed your thinking?

Conclusion

Summary

What good reason could there possibly be for not committing to a loving God who wants to bless us? Yet here are three reasons why we might hesitate to trust God with our lives.

1st Reason—Spiritual Maturity

A good God who wants our happiness also wants us to grow spiritually so we can experience more of his love, joy, and peace.

2nd Reason—Representing Him Well

What about when life is going well? Do we trust God in those times? Do we continue to seek his blessings when we're doing well without them?

3rd Reason—Correct Expectations

I've heard nonbelievers say they don't need God as their life is going fine without him. This disturbs me since it sounds like God exists for my convenience, to fix my problems, and to keep me happy. This view fails to acknowledge his sovereignty and his Lordship. This world isn't all there is, and life isn't about me.

On the Flying Trapeze

At times, living a Christian live may feel like a being on a flying trapeze, where we let go of our earthly comforts and securities and rely on God. Will we trust him when he calls us to life on the flying trapeze?

Discussion Question

1. Which reason resonates with you the most?

2. Do you have any further thoughts on anything in the book?

Acknowledgements

First and foremost I'd like to express my gratitude to God for the opportunities he has provided for me to write and for giving his people the Bible, without which I would have nothing to share.

The journey from idea to publication has been particularly long for this book, and many people have been part of the journey. I'm grateful to Omega Writers (Australia's Christian Writers Network) for their support and commitment to providing resources for Christian writers. Writing is a lonely venture, and I'm grateful to everyone who's ever asked me about my writing projects, particularly those who have helped me in a professional capacity.

I began reading Christian Living books as a young teenager and over the last fifty years have read hundreds of Christian books. I would like to acknowledge some of my favorite authors, which doesn't mean I agree with everything they teach, but they have challenged, clarified, and made me rethink my ideas: Dan Allender, Neil Anderson, Craig Blomberg, Mark Buchanan, Tony Campolo, Joanna Collicutt McGrath, John Mark Comer, Thomas Constable, Wayne Cordeiro, Larry Crabb, Suzanne de Dietrich, John Dickson, Michael Frost, Pete Greig, Selwyn Hughes, Phillip Keller, Timothy Keller, Krish Kandiah, Max Lucado, Floyd McClung, Scott McKnight, Brian McLaren, Don Miller, Beth Moore, Joyce Meyer, John Ortberg, Lucy Peppiatt, John Piper, Francine Rivers, David Seamands, Andy Stanley,

Lee Strobel, Alan J. Thompson, Frank Viola, Bruce Wilkinson, Kel Willis, and Philip Yancey.

Endnotes

10 Blessings of God

God Shares His Happiness

1. The Visual Bible, *Matthew*, directed by Regardt van den Bergh (Visual International, 1997), VHS.

2. Bruce Marchiano, *In the Footsteps of Jesus: One Man's Journey through the Life of Christ* (Eugene, OR: Harvest House, 1997).

3. C. S. Lewis, *Reflections on the Psalms* (New York, NY: Harvest Books, 1986), cited in John Piper, "Our Grand Obligation: Glorify God by Enjoying Him Forever," Desiring God, June 3, 2016, https://www.desiringgod.org/messages/our-grand-obligation

God Surprises

1. Thomas L. Constable, Dr. Constable's Expository Notes on John, John 2:6, StudyLight.org, accessed August 19, 2024, https://www.studylight.org/commentaries/eng/dcc/john-2.html

2. R. C. Sproul, *The Holiness of God* (Carol Stream, IL: Tyndale House, 1998), 124–126.

3. John Piper, "God Is Most Glorified in Us When We Are Most Satisfied in Him," Desiring God, October 13, 2012, https://www.desiringgod.org/messages/god-is-most-glorified-in-us-when-we-are-most-satisfied-in-him

God Frees

1. Gil Cann, "Up-to-the-Minute Forgiveness," (sermon, Nicholas Street Baptist Church, Geelong, Victoria, Australia, ca. 1981).

2. Thomas L. Constable, *Dr. Constable's Expository Notes on Acts,* Acts 15:20, StudyLight.org, accessed December 15, 2023, https://www.studylight.org/commentaries/eng/dcc/acts-15.html

God Identifies with Us

1. Billy Graham, "The Message," Billy Graham Evangelistic Association, accessed December 18, 2023, https://memorial.billygraham.org/the-message

2. Warren W. Wiersbe, *Be Courageous*, Luke 14–24 (Amersham-on-the-hill, England: Scripture Press Foundation, 1989), 29–32.

3. Mark Buchanan, *The Holy Wild: Trusting in the Character of God* (Sisters, OR: Multnomah Books, 2003), 113–116.

4. Warren W. Wiersbe, *Be Victorious*, Revelation (Amersham-on-the-hill, England: Scripture Press Foundation, 1985), 44.

5. Wiersbe, *Be Victorious*, 45.

6. A. W. Tozer, *And He Dwelt Among Us: Teachings from the Gospel of John* (Canada: ReadHowYouWant.com, Limited, 2010), 135.

God Loves

1. Daily Christian Quotes, "Blaise Pascal," January 15, 2014, https://www.dailychristianquote.com/?s=pascal

2. Geoffrey Johnstone, *The Gumtree Pulpit* (Melbourne, AUS: Geoffrey Johnstone, 2003), 170.

God Gives Hope

1. Robert Zemeckis, dir., *Cast Away* (Los Angeles: 20th Century Fox, 2000).

2. Stanford E. Murrell, *Twelve Men that Changed the World*, SoundDoctrine.net, accessed July 4, 2024, https://www.sounddoctrine.net/stanford/The%20Twelve%20Apostles.pdf, 43–44

3. Thomas L. Constable, *Dr. Constable's Expository Notes on Acts,* Acts 16:13, StudyLight.org, accessed December 15, 2023, https://www.studylight.org/commentaries/eng/dcc/acts-16.html

4. Katharine Tynan, "The Great Mercy," in *Flower of Youth: Poems in War Time* (London, UK: Sidgwick & Jackson, 1915).

5. Andrew Klavan, *The Great Good Thing: A Secular Jew Comes to Faith in Christ* (Nashville, TN: Thomas Nelson, 2016), 235.

God Has a Plan

1. Goodreads, "Bill Watterson > Quotes," accessed December 21, 2023, https://www.goodreads.com/author/quotes/13778.Bill_Watterson

2. Fern Neal Stocker, *Gladys Aylward* (Chicago, IL: Moody Press, 1988), 108.

3. Thomas L. Constable, *Dr. Constable's Expository Notes on Amos,* Historical Background, StudyLight.org, accessed December 15, 2023, https://www.studylight.org/commentaries/eng/dcc/amos.html

God Blesses

1. Harville Hendrix and Helen LaKelly, *Receiving Love: Transform Your Relationship by Letting Yourself Be Loved* (New York, NY: Atria, 2004).

2. Craig L. Blomberg, *Interpreting the Parables* (Downers Grove, IL: InterVarsity Press, 1990), 273.

3. Thomas L. Constable, *Dr. Constable's Expository Notes on Matthew*, Matthew 5:6, StudyLight.org, accessed July 20, 2024, https://www.studylight.org/commentaries/eng/dcc/matthew-5.html

God Gives Peace

1. Watchman Nee, "November 15th," in *A Table in the Wilderness: Daily Meditations* (Eastbourne, UK: Victory Press, 1969).

2. Thomas L. Constable, *Dr. Constable's Expository Notes on Job,* Date, StudyLight.org, accessed December 23, 2023, https://www.studylight.org/commentaries/eng/dcc/job.html

3. W. Oscar Thompson Jr., *Concentric Circles of Concern: Seven Stages for Making Disciples* (Nashville, TN: Broadman Press, 1981), 165.

God Overcomes

1. *Oceans Eleven*, directed by Steven Soderbergh (Warner Bros Pictures, 2001).

2. Saint Teresa, cited in Lee Strobel, *The Case for Faith: A Journalist Investigates the Toughest Objections to Christianity* (Grand Rapids, MI: Zondervan, 2000), 47.

3. C. S. Lewis, *The Silver Chair* (London: HarperCollins, 2001), 200.

4. Sheldon Vanauken, *A Severe Mercy: A Story of Faith, Tragedy, and Triumph* (United States: Bantam Books, 1979), 211.

Conclusion

1. Thomas L. Constable, *Dr. Constable's Expository Notes on Isaiah*, Isaiah 10:24–27, StudyLight.org, accessed December 26, 2023, https://www.studylight.org/commentaries/eng/dcc/isaiah-10.html

2. *The Westminster Shorter Catechism* (Philadelphia, PA.: Presbyterian Board of Publication and Sabbath-School work, 1897), 7.

Next book coming in 2026

The next book in Susan's Christian living series is due for release in 2026. Look out for the title, it will start with the number 10.

In the meantime sign up for Susan's newsletter and receive a weekly dose of grace and inspiration, plus regular updates on her writing progress.

www.susanbarneswriter.com

www.ingramcontent.com/pod-product-compliance
Lightning Source LLC
Chambersburg PA
CBHW020526080526
44583CB00013B/757